DRAWING
FIGURES

by Michel **Lauricella**

rockynook

I would like to thank Nathalie Tournillon, who suggested this collection to me; Hélène Raviart, for our productive discussions; and Camille Monin, for the editing and rewriting of many passages that are now much clearer.

All illustrations are by the author, except for figure 1 on page 5: photo SCALA, Florence: Courtesy of the Ministero Beni e Att. Culturali e del Turismo, Dist. GrandpalaisRmn / image Scala

DRAWING: Figures
Michel Lauricella

Editor: Jocelyn Howell
Project manager: Lisa Brazieal
Marketing manager: Koryn Olage
Layout and type: Anthony Paular Design
Front cover and interior design: Sophie Charbonnel
Cover production: Anthony Paular Design
Cover illustrations: Michel Lauricella
Translation: Marie Deer

ISBN: 979-8-88814-361-2
(1st printing, April 2025)
© 2025 Michel Lauricella

Rocky Nook Inc.
1010 B Street, Suite 350
San Rafael, CA 94901
USA

Original French title: *Les personnages par Michel Lauricella*
© 2024, Éditions Eyrolles, Paris, France

Distributed in the UK and Europe by Publishers Group UK
Distributed in the U.S. and all other territories by Publishers Group West

All rights reserved. No part of the material protected by this copyright notice may be reproduced or utilized in any form, electronic or mechanical, including photocopying, recording, or by any information storage and retrieval system, without written permission of the publisher.

Many of the designations in this book used by manufacturers and sellers to distinguish their products are claimed as trademarks of their respective companies. Where those designations appear in this book, and Rocky Nook was aware of a trademark claim, the designations have been printed in caps or initial caps. All product names and services identified throughout this book are used in editorial fashion only and for the benefit of such companies with no intention of infringement of the trademark. They are not intended to convey endorsement or other affiliation with this book.

While reasonable care has been exercised in the preparation of this book, the publisher and author assume no responsibility for errors or omissions, or for damages resulting from the use of the information contained herein or from the use of the discs or programs that may accompany it.

This book is printed on acid-free paper.

Printed in China

Contents

Introduction

Figure drawing can be done in many ways. Give yourself permission to use all different kinds of models: photographs (from magazines, newspapers, or the internet), copies (of drawings, paintings, sculptures), your family (reading, knitting, watching TV, etc.), friends, strangers (in cafés and other public places), yourself (in a mirror for a self-portrait, your free hand, or your feet!). In short, it's all good, as long as you're practicing, because it is better to have a light but regular practice (even a few minutes gleaned here and there) than wait forever until all the conditions are perfect.

When we start, we are often drawn to resemblance, a term that usually means "the desire to approach a photographic rendering." Of course, drawing is not limited to this. It offers you great freedom of execution, which makes many expressive experiences possible. Transformations and deformations, whether voluntary or not [column 2] (accept the awkwardness!) are very often much more evocative.

Unfortunately, the format of this book means that I can only present so much. This book is primarily intended for those who are just starting out in drawing and who want to draw realistic or semi-realistic human characters, along the lines of many comics and graphic novels, animated films, and video games. I hope you will enjoy copying or just being inspired by my drawings, but most of all, do not lose sight of the fact that everything is allowed! Remember that drawing is a wonderful form of expression because of its simplicity (all you need are a pencil and a piece of paper), as well as an excellent mode of observation, which requires us to take our time. Remember, too, that drawing always involves making choices, and that those choices are infinite. And finally, keep in mind that all tools, all formats, and all materials (sketchbooks, plain notebooks, etc.) are welcome, and that each of these will lead you to see things differently.

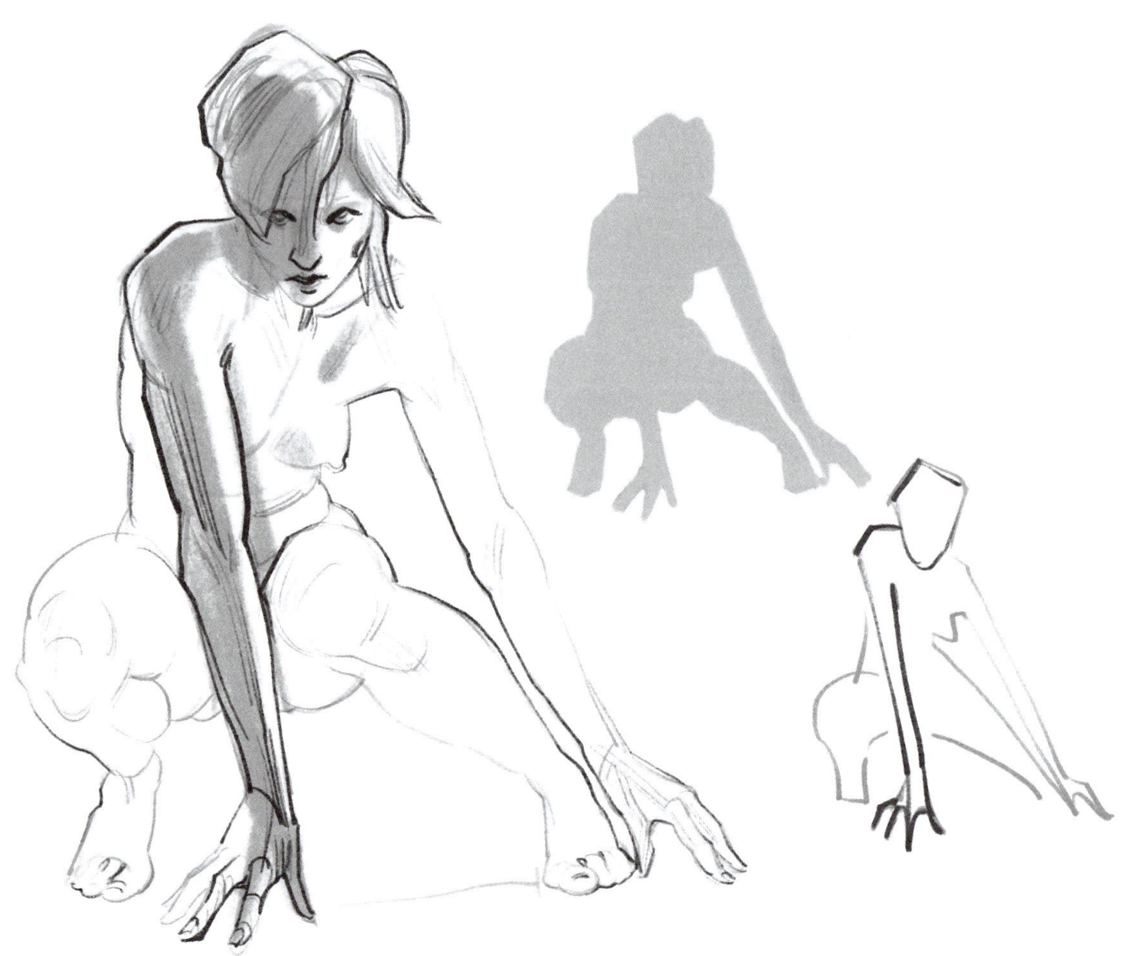

Bodily Proportions

Fig. 1 There are many different canonical rules for proportions. I have chosen one of the best-known, by Leonardo da Vinci, which is very easy to memorize:
- our wingspan is equal to our height (this is, of course, just a general rule, and depending on the width of your shoulders, your wingspan might be less than or greater than your height);
- the height of a body is generally equivalent to the height of eight heads stacked on top of each other;
- the halfway point of the body comes at the level of the pelvis (above the genitals); the quarter point comes at the level of the knee joint.

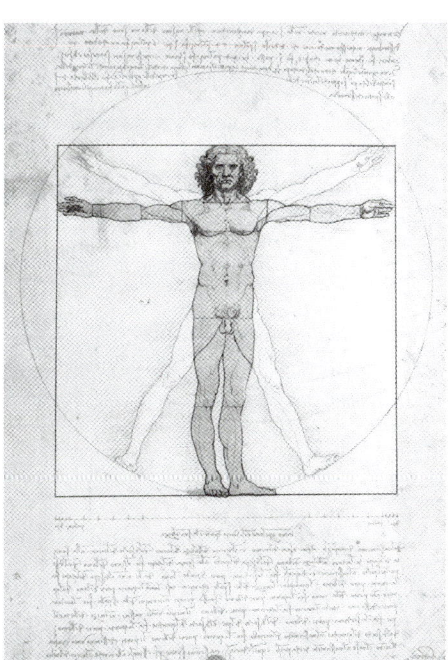

Fig. 1

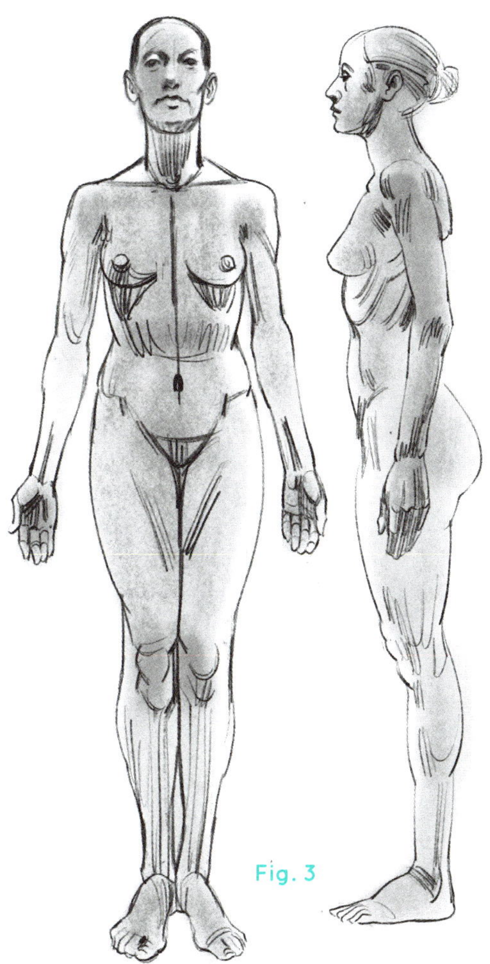

Fig. 3 When the arms are along the sides of the body, the hand usually reaches to mid-thigh.

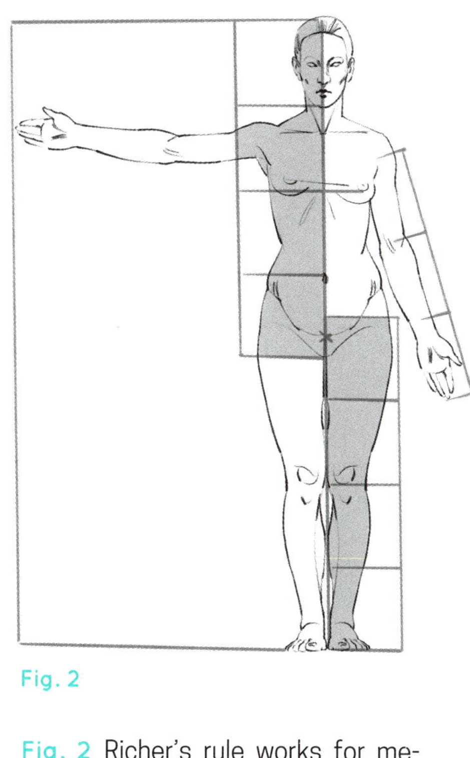

Fig. 2

Fig. 2 Richer's rule works for medium heights. To apply it, just make the two halves of the previous rule (height of body = eight heads) overlap by half of a head height.

Fig. 3

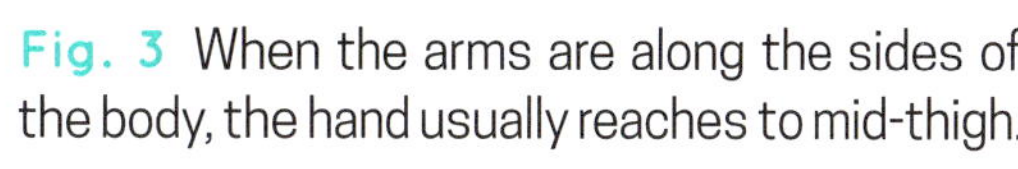

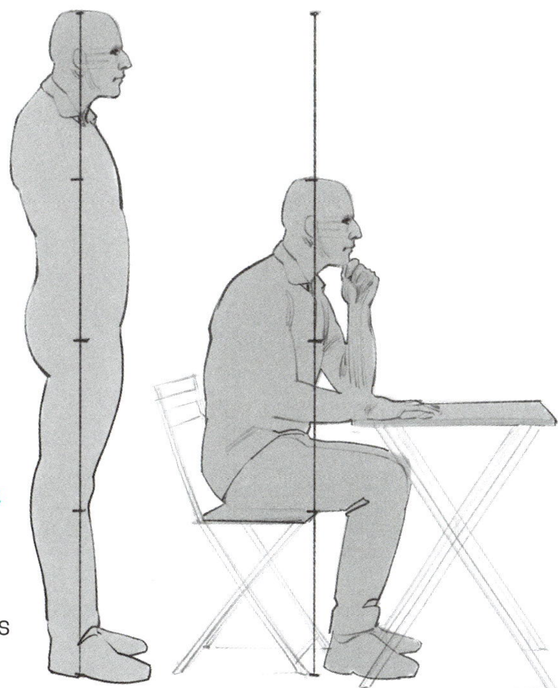

Fig. 5

Fig. 4

Fig. 4 A seated person loses a quarter of their height.

Fig. 5 The reason we can sit on our heels is that the thigh is the same length as the lower leg and the foot together.

Head Proportions

Fig. 1 The eyes are placed at the halfway point of the face. The height of the nose, if transferred to the top of the face, would correspond to the hairline, and if transferred to the lower half, would correspond to the point of the chin. Here, the ear is at the same height as the nose, and in profile, it is at the halfway point, just behind the jaw joint (following da Vinci).

Fig. 2 Adult and newborn (following G. Bammes; see the resources on p. 32).

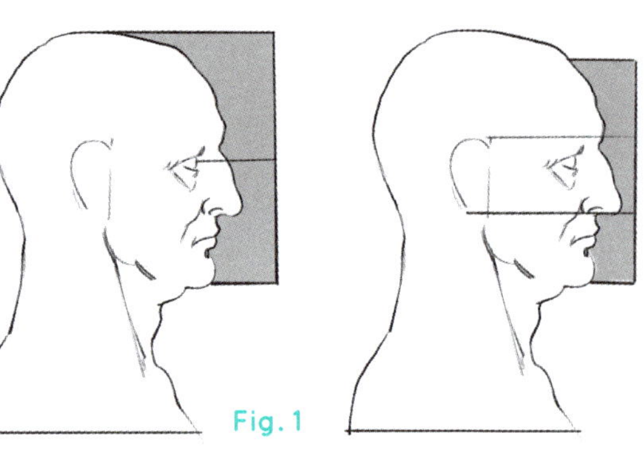

Fig. 1

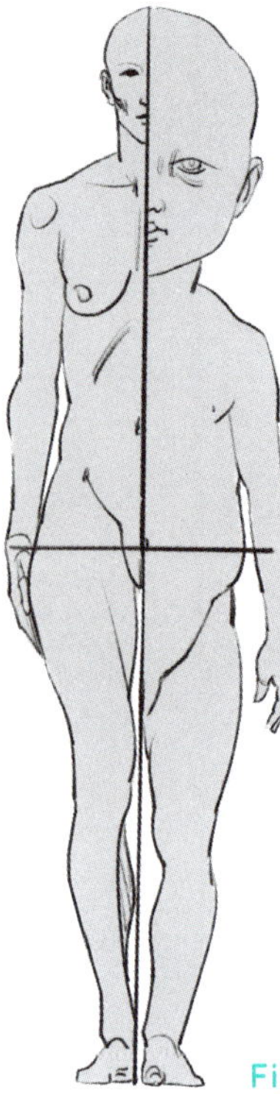

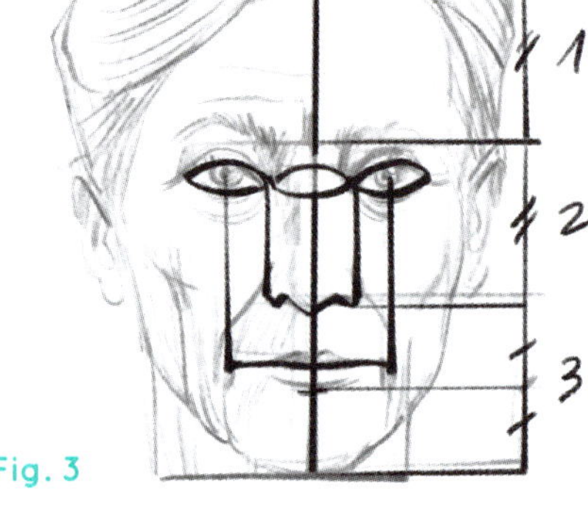

Fig. 2

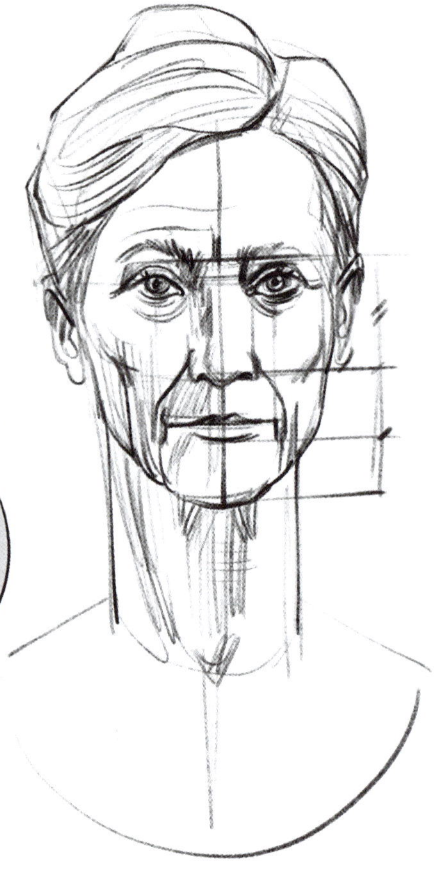

Fig. 3

Fig. 3 A third eye could be slipped in between the two eyes. The width of the nose can coincide with this proportion, whereas the corners of the lips are directly below the middle of the eyes. However, these are only mnemonic tricks; the variations are endless, and asymmetry reigns in the details!

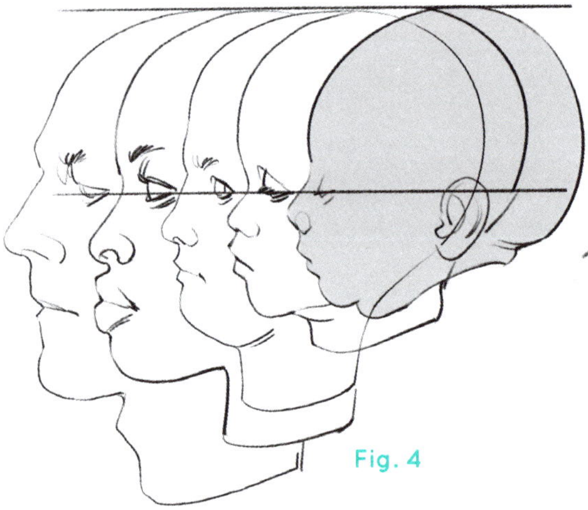

Fig. 4

Fig. 4 These profiles are aligned along the same height between the eye and the top of the skull. But note here that the proportions are not the same: the skull of a newborn is usually 35 cm in circumference, while an adult skull is about 55 cm or 60 cm around. The absence of teeth, the presence of milk teeth, and then the appearance of the permanent teeth obviously have a strong impact on head sizes.

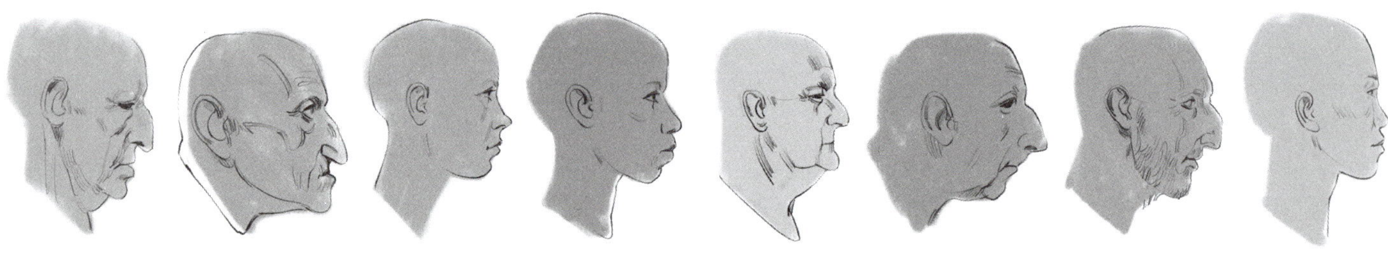

Hair

Fig. 5 It is worth paying attention to the fact that we usually imagine the ear as being closer to the eyes than it actually is. Is this because of how we see our face in a mirror, which foreshortens this distance? A large head of hair can also mislead us.

Figs. 6 and 7 Don't forget the shape of the skull underneath the head of hair. Its roundness can be expressed through the play of light and, if the texture of the hair allows it, by how the strands of hair are drawn.

Figs. 8 and 9 Hair loss often occurs according to these patterns, which are well-known in cosmetic surgery. Hair loss starting at the crown at the back of the head (fig. 8) is a classic form of baldness.

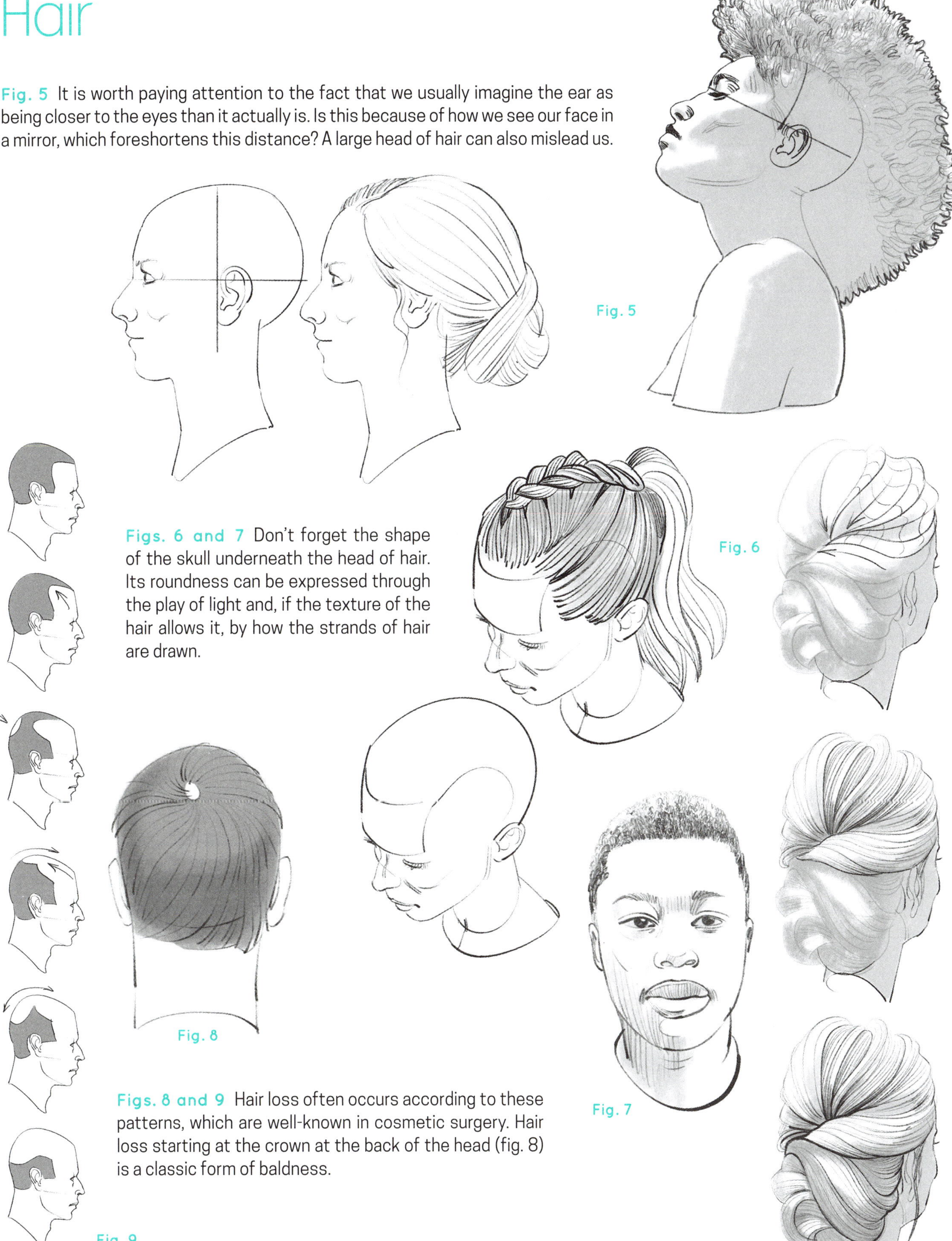

Eyes and Nose

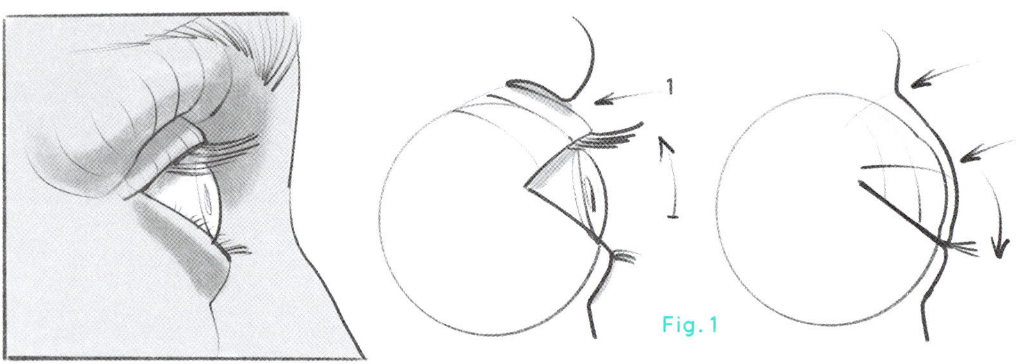

Fig. 1 Opening and closing of the eyelids. The line of the eyelid fold (1) can be seen on the upper eyelid when it is closed.

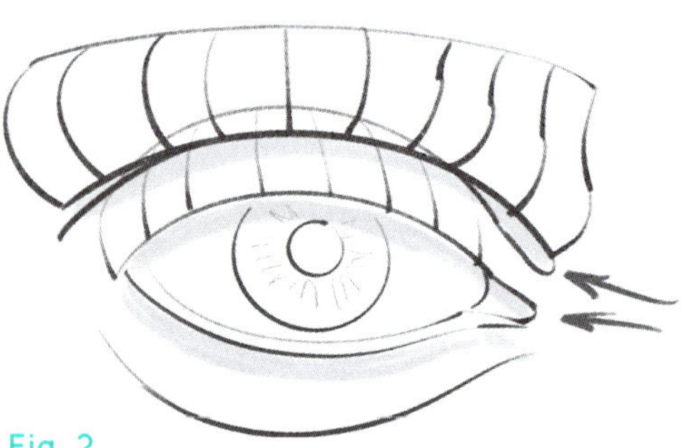

Fig. 2

Fig. 2 The eyelid fold can be positioned higher and lower, and sometimes even covers the upper eyelid.

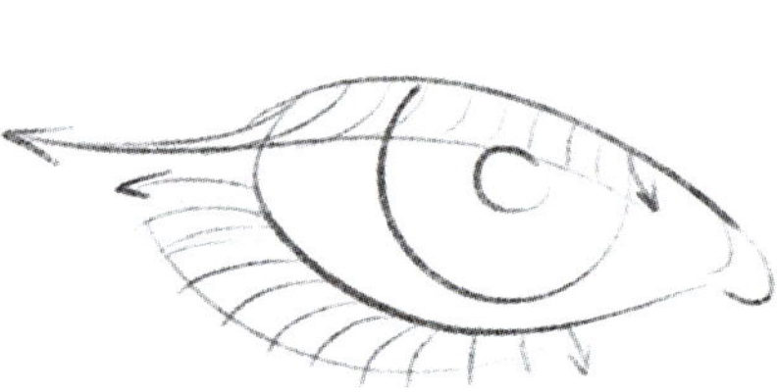

Fig. 3

Fig. 3 The eyebrows cast a protective shadow over the eyes and act like a sensitive filter.

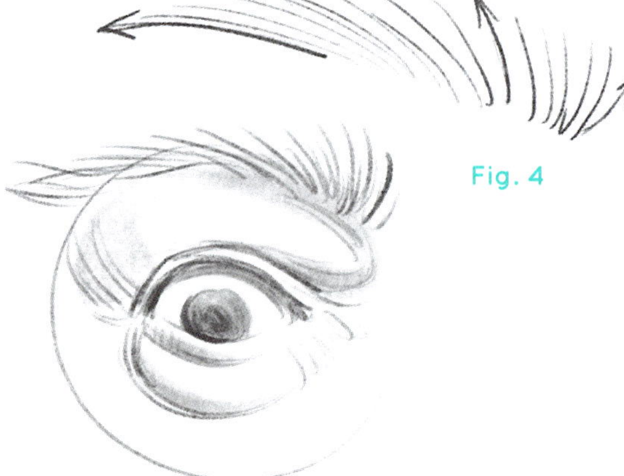

Fig. 4

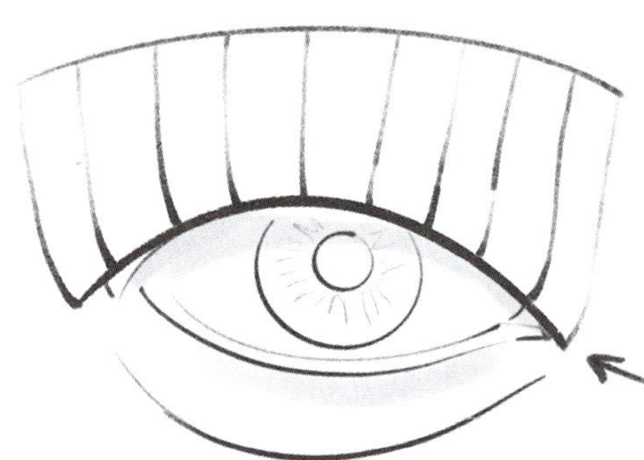

Fig. 4 At the inside end, the "head" of the eyebrow bursts, or radiates outward. Beginning there, the hairs are inclined toward its "tail" at the other end.

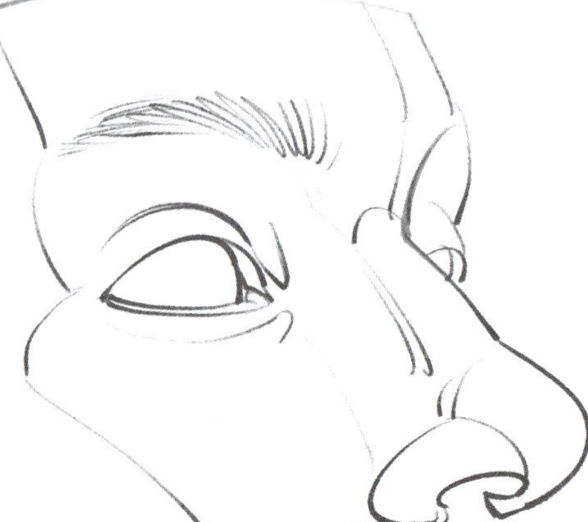

Fig. 5 The upper lip appears to be suspended from the nasal cartilages. Two fleshy lines outline the hollow under the nose (the philtrum).

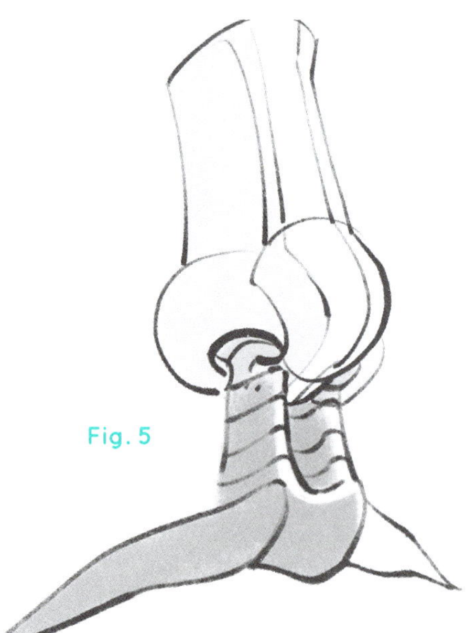

Fig. 5

Mouth and Ears

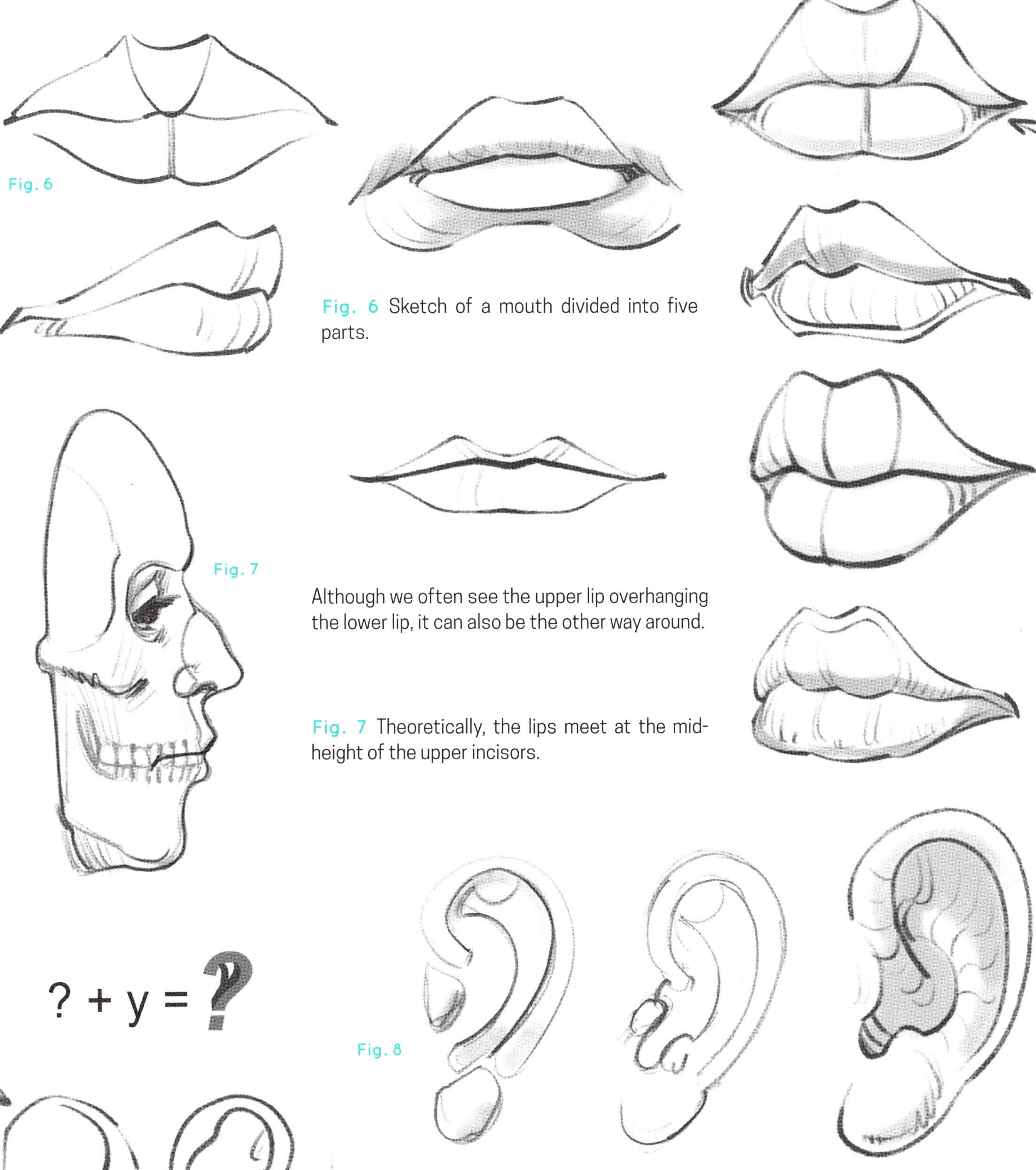

Fig. 6 Sketch of a mouth divided into five parts.

Although we often see the upper lip overhanging the lower lip, it can also be the other way around.

Fig. 7 Theoretically, the lips meet at the mid-height of the upper incisors.

Fig. 8 Mnemonic diagram of an ear (following the artist Norman Lemay).

Fig. 9 The lobe can be either free or largely attached, and the edges of the ear can be more or less hemmed, or curled.

Hands

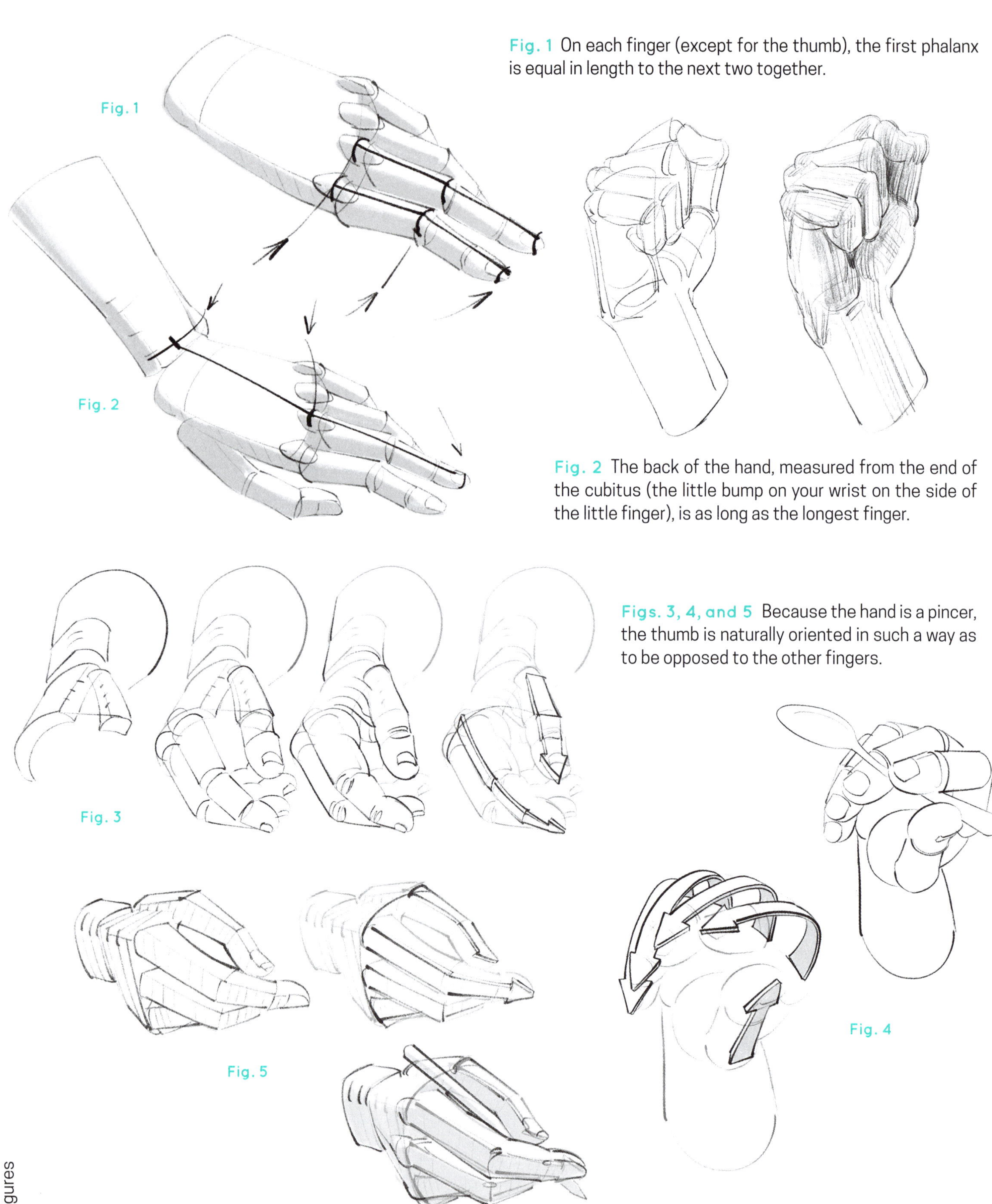

Fig. 1 On each finger (except for the thumb), the first phalanx is equal in length to the next two together.

Fig. 2 The back of the hand, measured from the end of the cubitus (the little bump on your wrist on the side of the little finger), is as long as the longest finger.

Figs. 3, 4, and 5 Because the hand is a pincer, the thumb is naturally oriented in such a way as to be opposed to the other fingers.

Feet

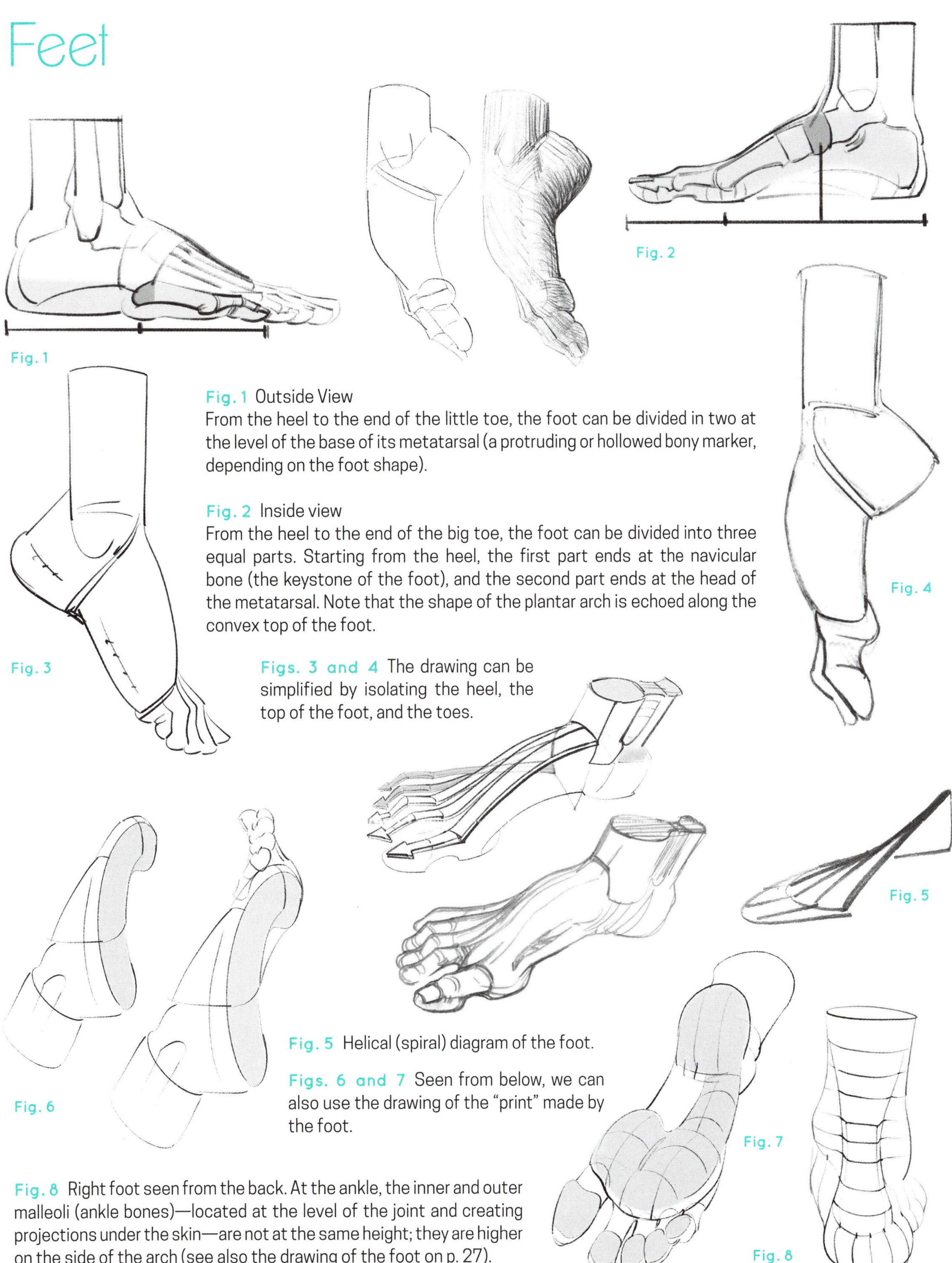

Fig. 1

Fig. 2

Fig. 3

Fig. 4

Fig. 1 Outside View
From the heel to the end of the little toe, the foot can be divided in two at the level of the base of its metatarsal (a protruding or hollowed bony marker, depending on the foot shape).

Fig. 2 Inside view
From the heel to the end of the big toe, the foot can be divided into three equal parts. Starting from the heel, the first part ends at the navicular bone (the keystone of the foot), and the second part ends at the head of the metatarsal. Note that the shape of the plantar arch is echoed along the convex top of the foot.

Figs. 3 and 4 The drawing can be simplified by isolating the heel, the top of the foot, and the toes.

Fig. 5

Fig. 6

Fig. 7

Fig. 8

Fig. 5 Helical (spiral) diagram of the foot.

Figs. 6 and 7 Seen from below, we can also use the drawing of the "print" made by the foot.

Fig. 8 Right foot seen from the back. At the ankle, the inner and outer malleoli (ankle bones)—located at the level of the joint and creating projections under the skin—are not at the same height; they are higher on the side of the arch (see also the drawing of the foot on p. 27).

The Skeleton

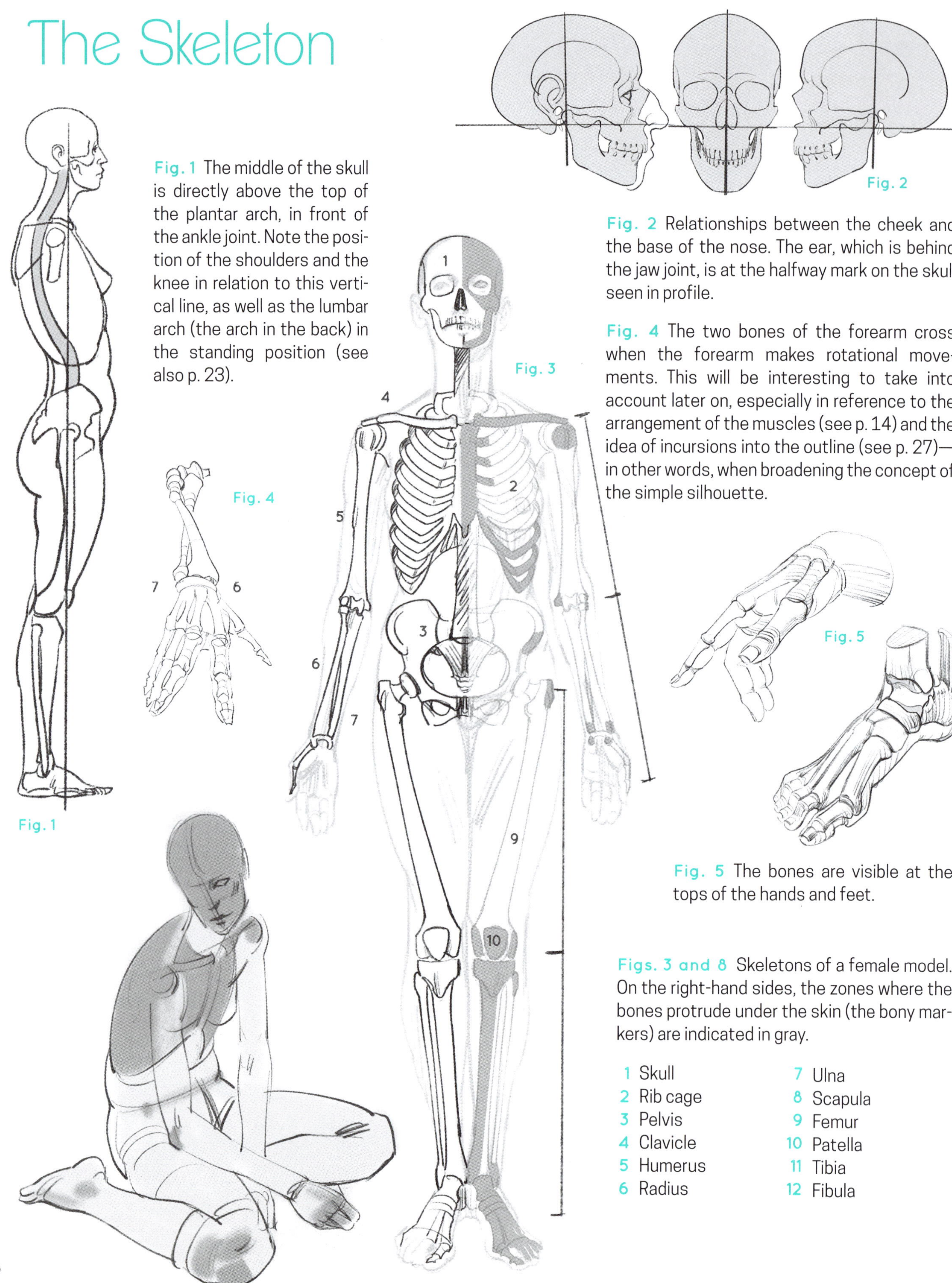

Fig. 1 The middle of the skull is directly above the top of the plantar arch, in front of the ankle joint. Note the position of the shoulders and the knee in relation to this vertical line, as well as the lumbar arch (the arch in the back) in the standing position (see also p. 23).

Fig. 2 Relationships between the cheek and the base of the nose. The ear, which is behind the jaw joint, is at the halfway mark on the skull seen in profile.

Fig. 4 The two bones of the forearm cross when the forearm makes rotational movements. This will be interesting to take into account later on, especially in reference to the arrangement of the muscles (see p. 14) and the idea of incursions into the outline (see p. 27)—in other words, when broadening the concept of the simple silhouette.

Fig. 5 The bones are visible at the tops of the hands and feet.

Figs. 3 and 8 Skeletons of a female model. On the right-hand sides, the zones where the bones protrude under the skin (the bony markers) are indicated in gray.

1	Skull	7	Ulna
2	Rib cage	8	Scapula
3	Pelvis	9	Femur
4	Clavicle	10	Patella
5	Humerus	11	Tibia
6	Radius	12	Fibula

Bony Markers

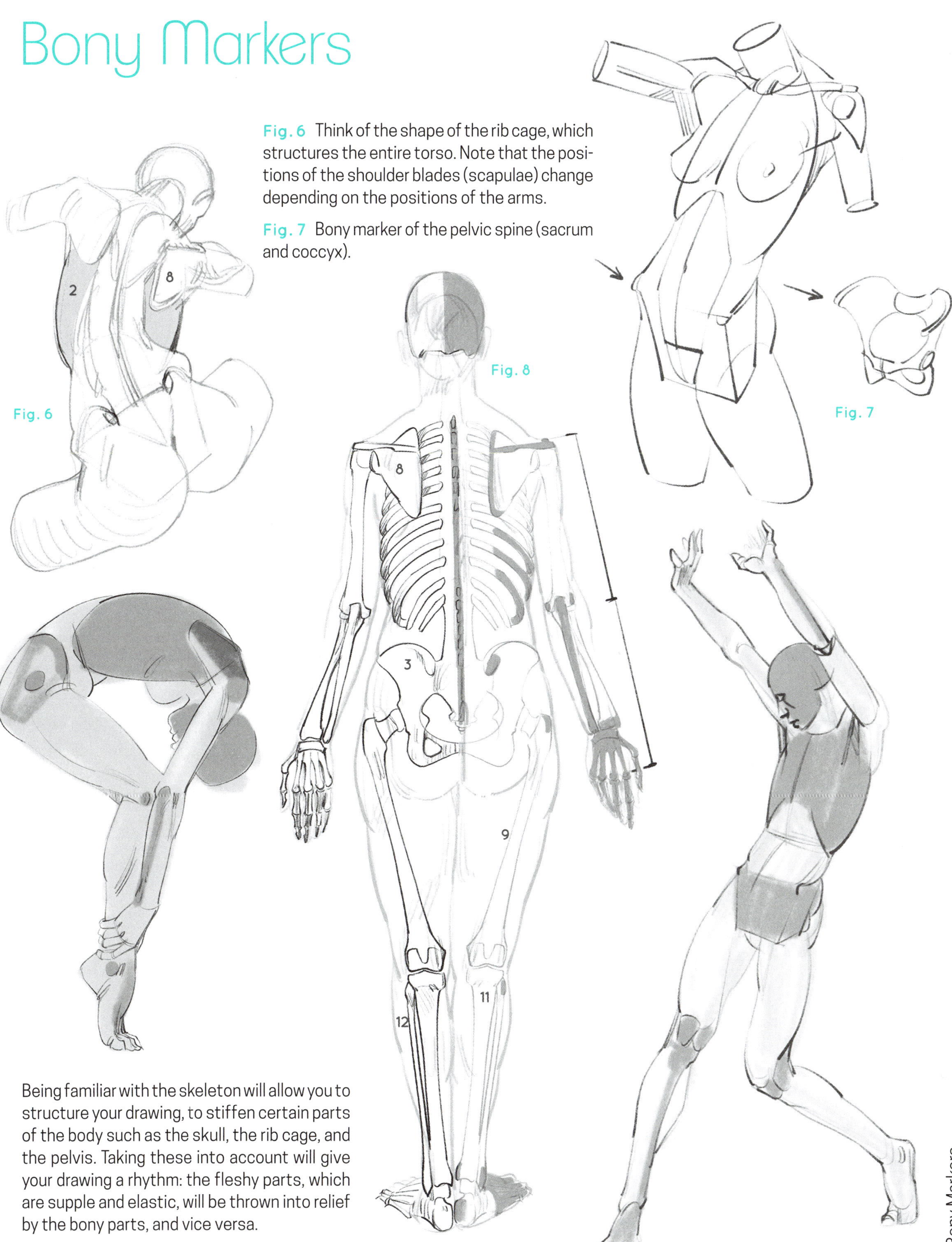

Fig. 6 Think of the shape of the rib cage, which structures the entire torso. Note that the positions of the shoulder blades (scapulae) change depending on the positions of the arms.

Fig. 7 Bony marker of the pelvic spine (sacrum and coccyx).

Being familiar with the skeleton will allow you to structure your drawing, to stiffen certain parts of the body such as the skull, the rib cage, and the pelvis. Taking these into account will give your drawing a rhythm: the fleshy parts, which are supple and elastic, will be thrown into relief by the bony parts, and vice versa.

Muscles

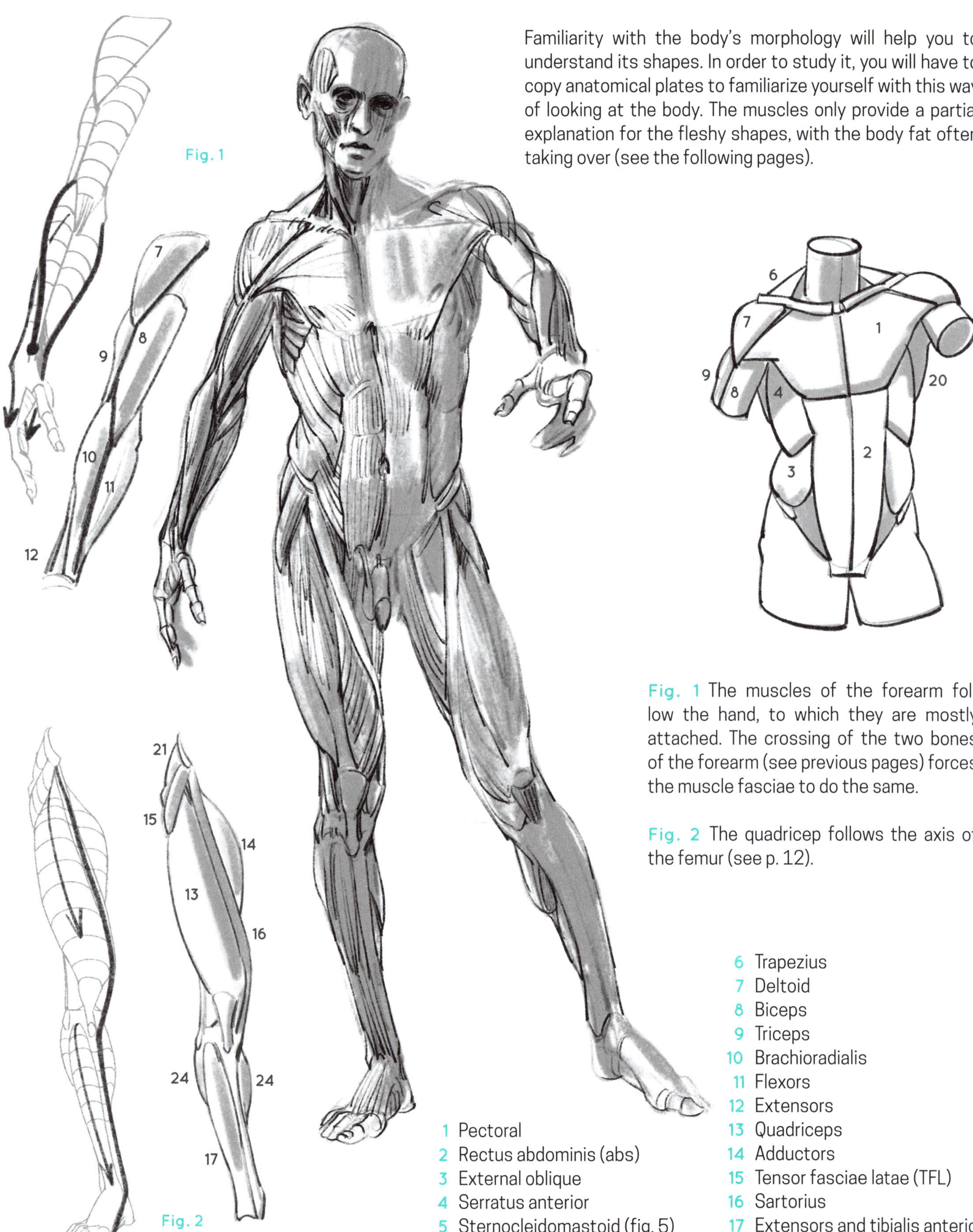

Familiarity with the body's morphology will help you to understand its shapes. In order to study it, you will have to copy anatomical plates to familiarize yourself with this way of looking at the body. The muscles only provide a partial explanation for the fleshy shapes, with the body fat often taking over (see the following pages).

Fig. 1 The muscles of the forearm follow the hand, to which they are mostly attached. The crossing of the two bones of the forearm (see previous pages) forces the muscle fasciae to do the same.

Fig. 2 The quadricep follows the axis of the femur (see p. 12).

1 Pectoral
2 Rectus abdominis (abs)
3 External oblique
4 Serratus anterior
5 Sternocleidomastoid (fig. 5)
6 Trapezius
7 Deltoid
8 Biceps
9 Triceps
10 Brachioradialis
11 Flexors
12 Extensors
13 Quadriceps
14 Adductors
15 Tensor fasciae latae (TFL)
16 Sartorius
17 Extensors and tibialis anterior

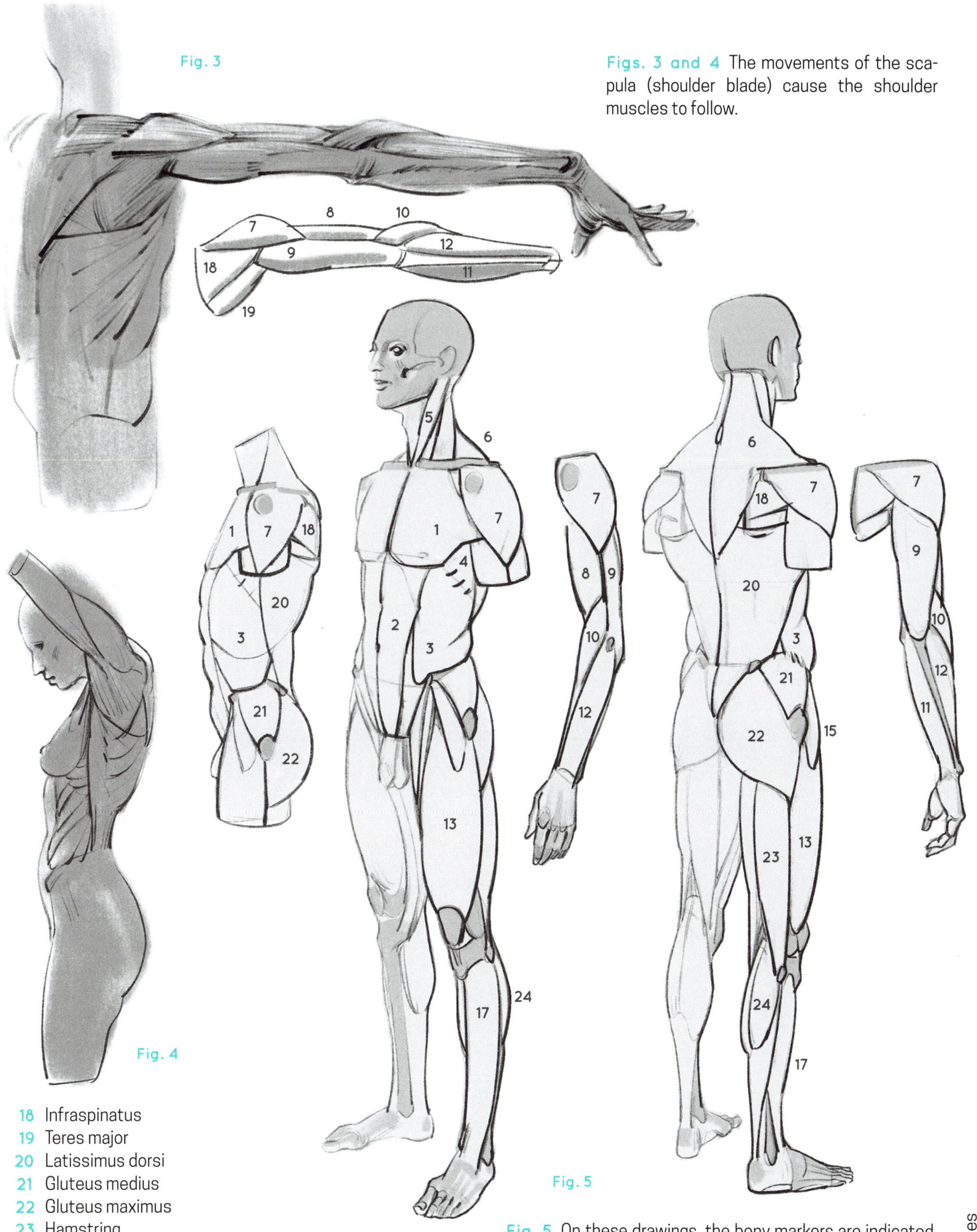

Figs. 3 and 4 The movements of the scapula (shoulder blade) cause the shoulder muscles to follow.

18 Infraspinatus
19 Teres major
20 Latissimus dorsi
21 Gluteus medius
22 Gluteus maximus
23 Hamstring
24 Gastrocnemius

Fig. 5 On these drawings, the bony markers are indicated in dark gray (see also pp. 12 and 13).

Skin and Fat

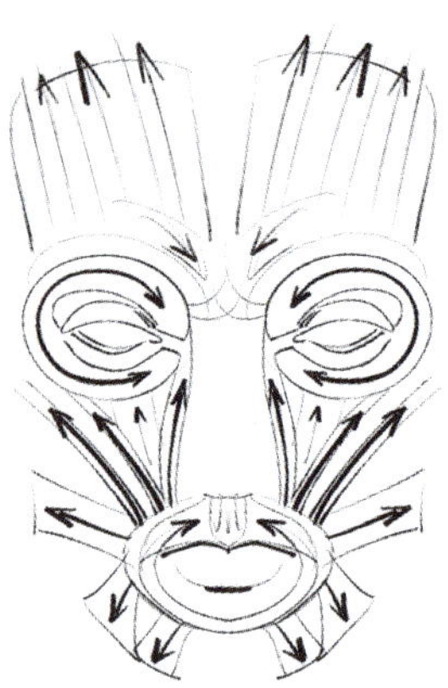

Fig. 1

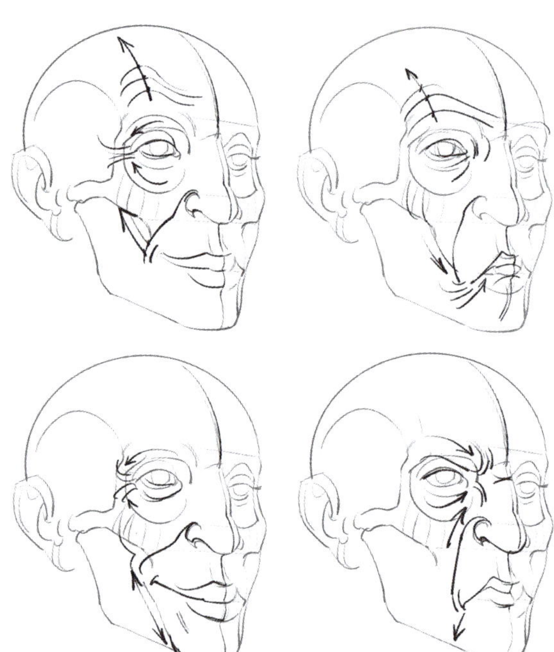

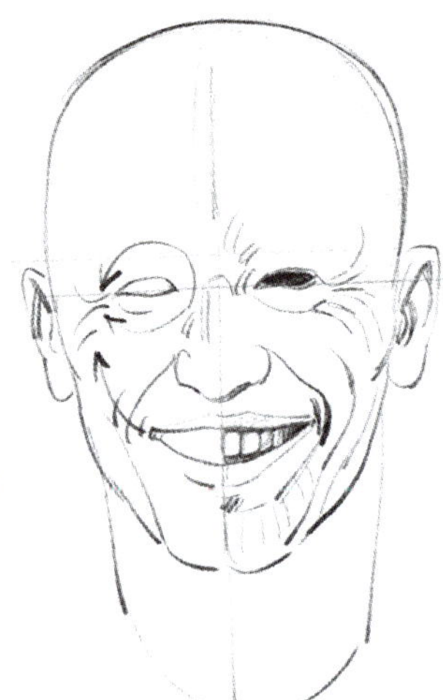

Fig. 1 The muscles of the face adhere to the skin and most of them radiate around and out from the mouth. When they contract, they shorten and pull the skin along with them, creating perpendicular folds in the direction of their fibers.

The skeleton and the musculature by themselves are not enough to explain all of the shapes of the body. Nor does fat create a simple uniform veil over the entire silhouette; instead, it has a variable thickness depending on the part of the body.

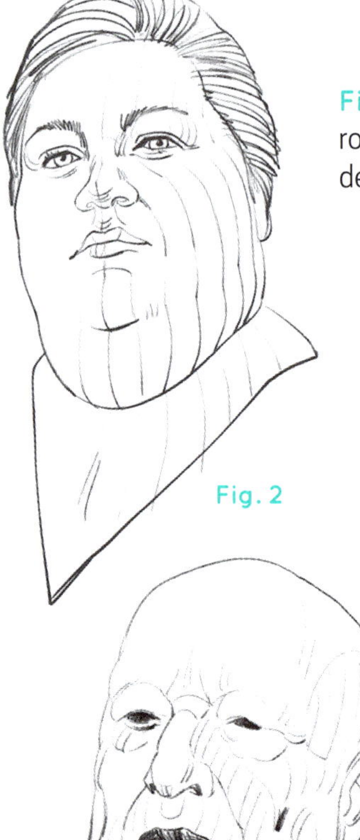

Fig. 2

Figs. 2 and 3 The shapes can be simplified and rounded, but with age, the skin loses its elasticity, develops folds, and is subject to gravity.

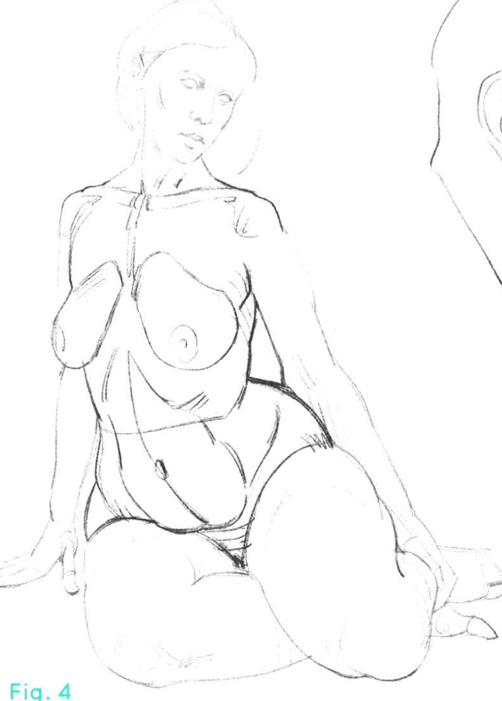

Fig. 3

Fig. 4

Fig. 4 The fat of the breast protects the mammary gland and is commonly found around the nipple in either sex. Fat develops more easily around the abdomen, and surrounds the buttocks.

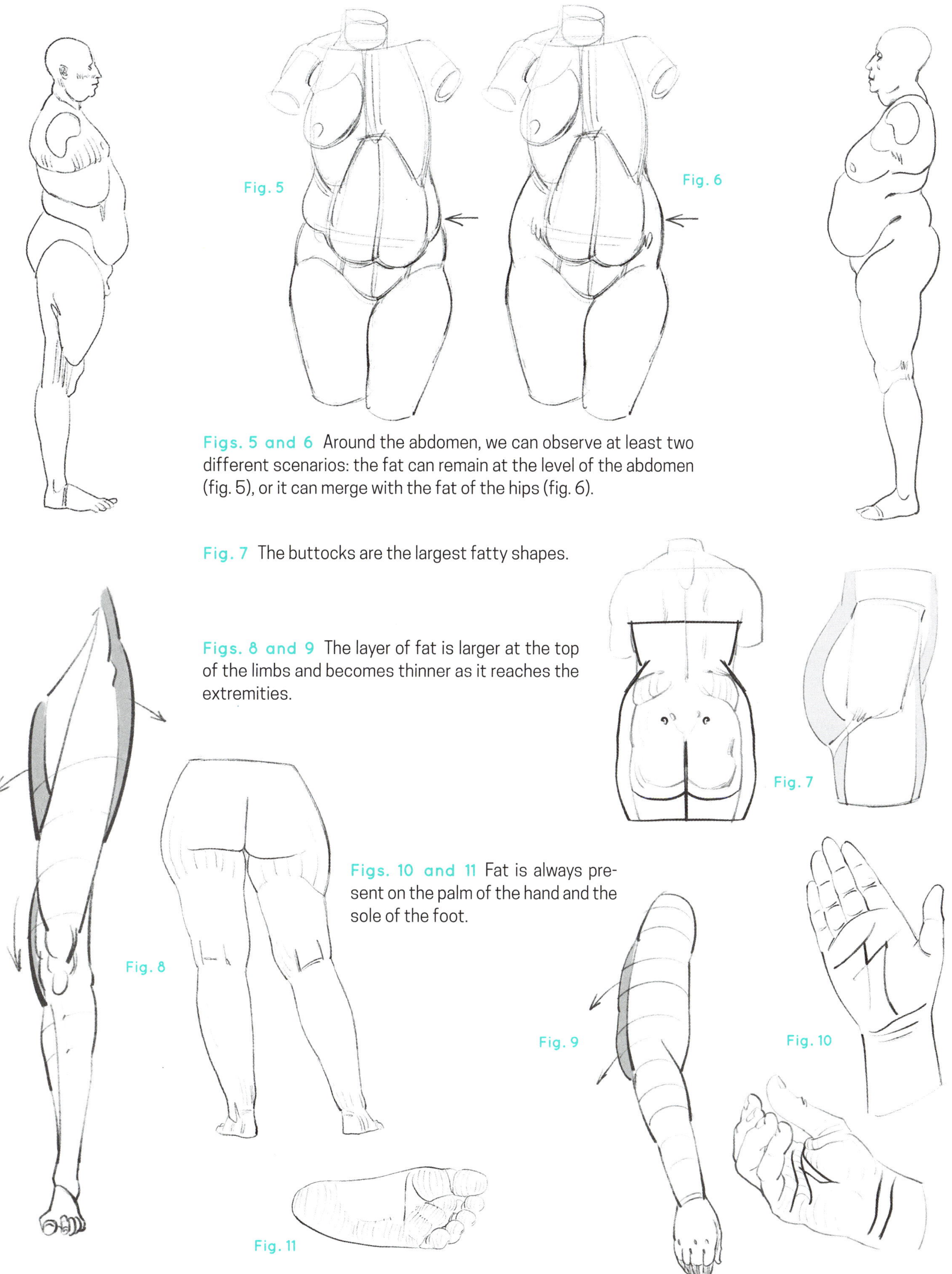

Figs. 5 and 6 Around the abdomen, we can observe at least two different scenarios: the fat can remain at the level of the abdomen (fig. 5), or it can merge with the fat of the hips (fig. 6).

Fig. 7 The buttocks are the largest fatty shapes.

Figs. 8 and 9 The layer of fat is larger at the top of the limbs and becomes thinner as it reaches the extremities.

Figs. 10 and 11 Fat is always present on the palm of the hand and the sole of the foot.

Simplified Shapes

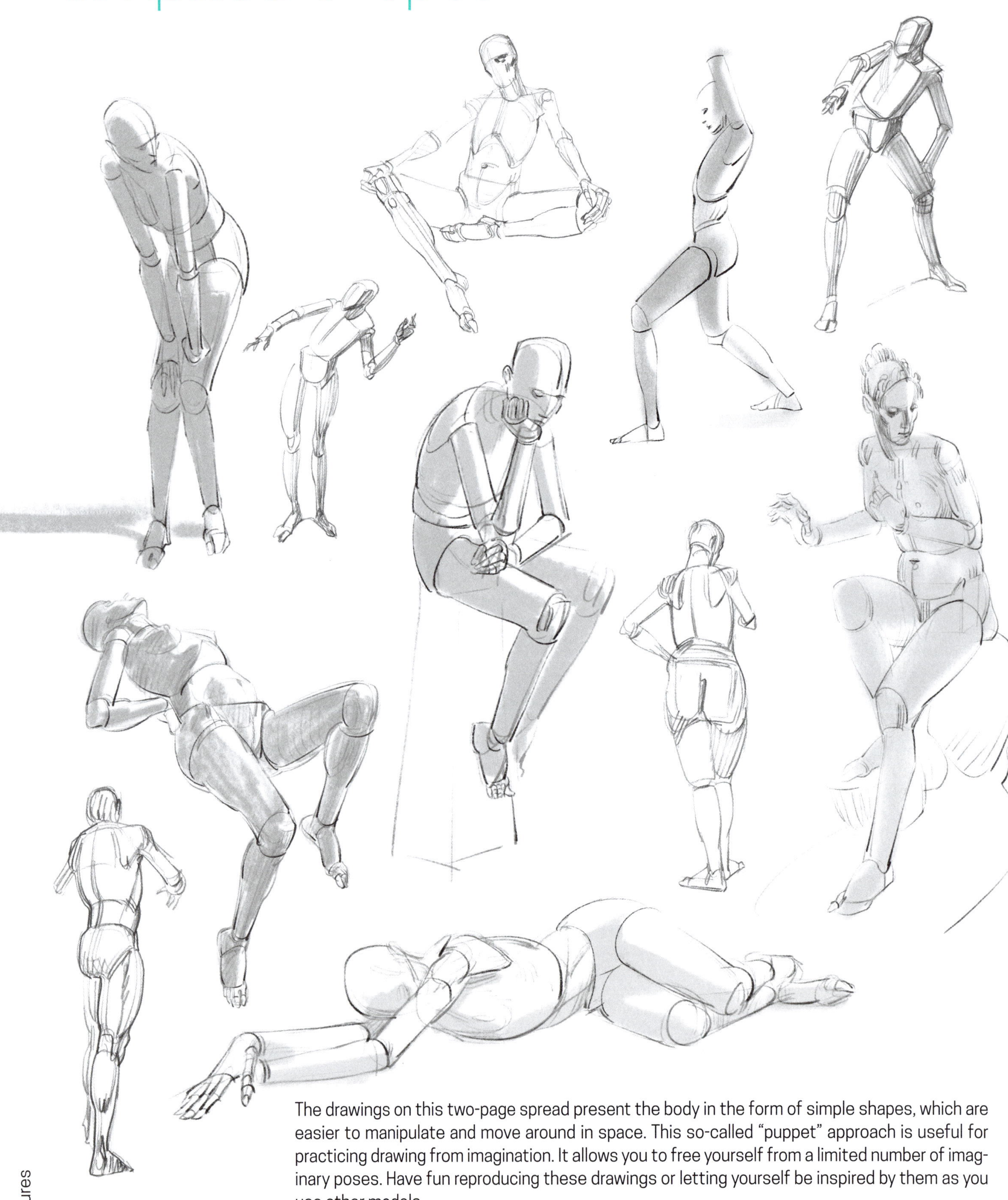

The drawings on this two-page spread present the body in the form of simple shapes, which are easier to manipulate and move around in space. This so-called "puppet" approach is useful for practicing drawing from imagination. It allows you to free yourself from a limited number of imaginary poses. Have fun reproducing these drawings or letting yourself be inspired by them as you use other models.

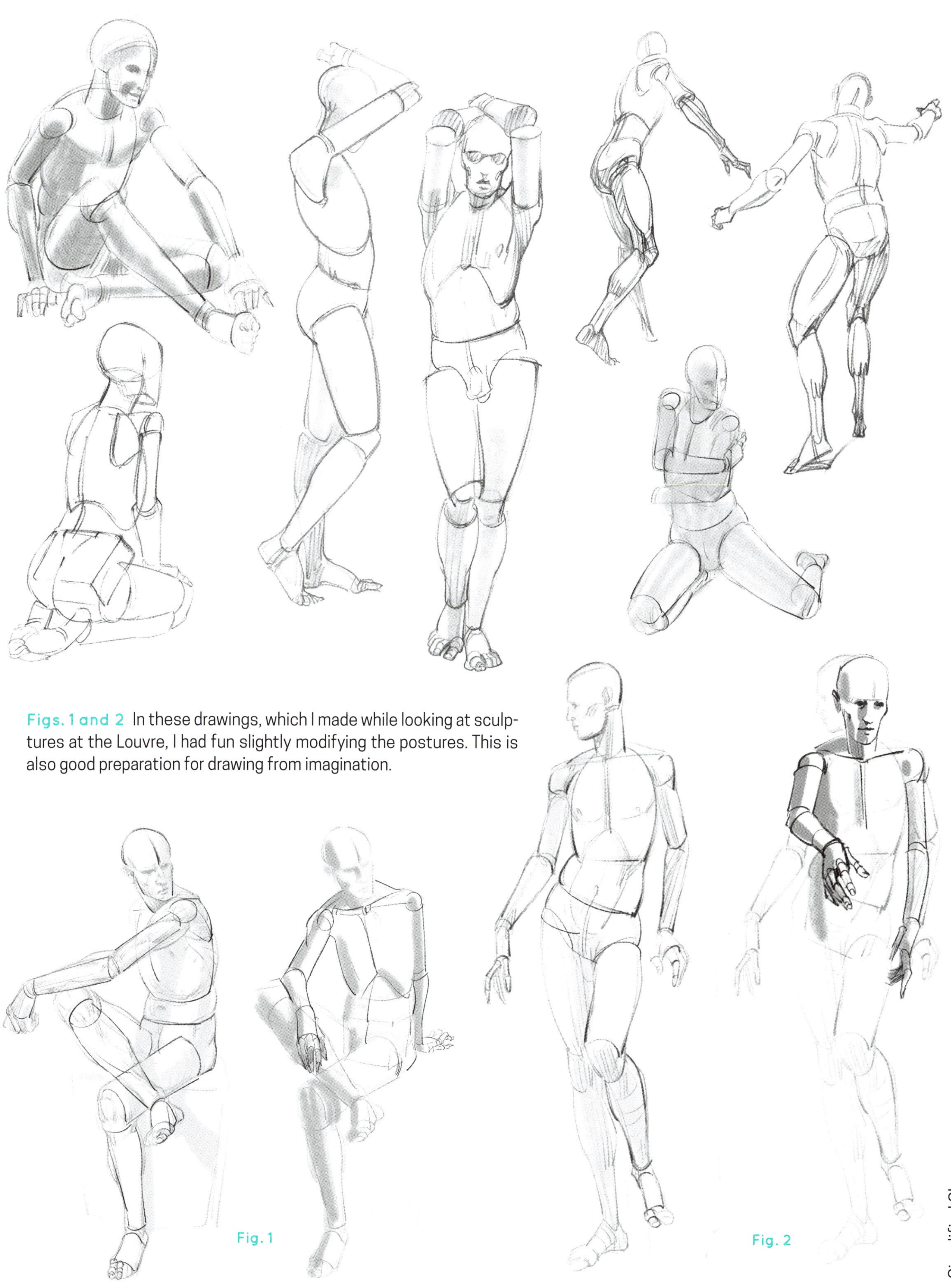

Figs. 1 and 2 In these drawings, which I made while looking at sculptures at the Louvre, I had fun slightly modifying the postures. This is also good preparation for drawing from imagination.

Fig. 1

Fig. 2

Silhouettes

Your task is now to train your eyes (and your hand!) to concentrate on the big picture, or global vision—to fight against the natural, but risky, tendency to start with the details when you draw. Why talk about risks? When you are starting out, you may have trouble composing your image (your drawing will be too small or too big compared to the format), not have enough time to finish, or have trouble keeping the overall proportions. Thus, it is easier to position the details later, on an overall view that you have already sketched in, even if this might seem counterintuitive at first.

Take a large implement (such as a marker, blunt pencil, finger, cloth and charcoal, etc.) and try to draw a silhouette by filling in its segments, rather than drawing its outlines and then coloring or filling it in. Feel free to blend the body segments into a single mass where they overlap. Then, inside these silhouettes, you can add details using lines.

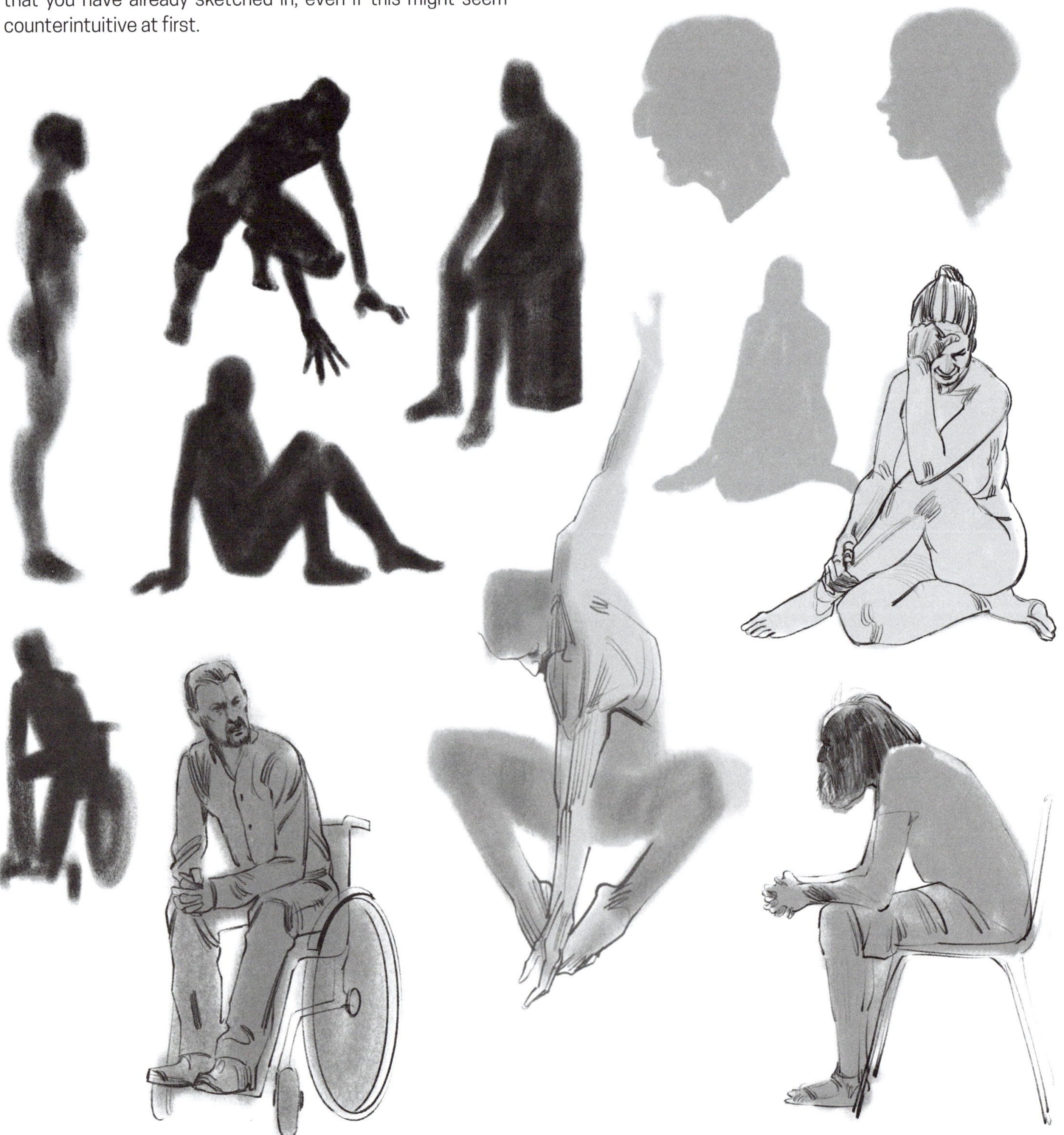

Filled and Empty Spaces

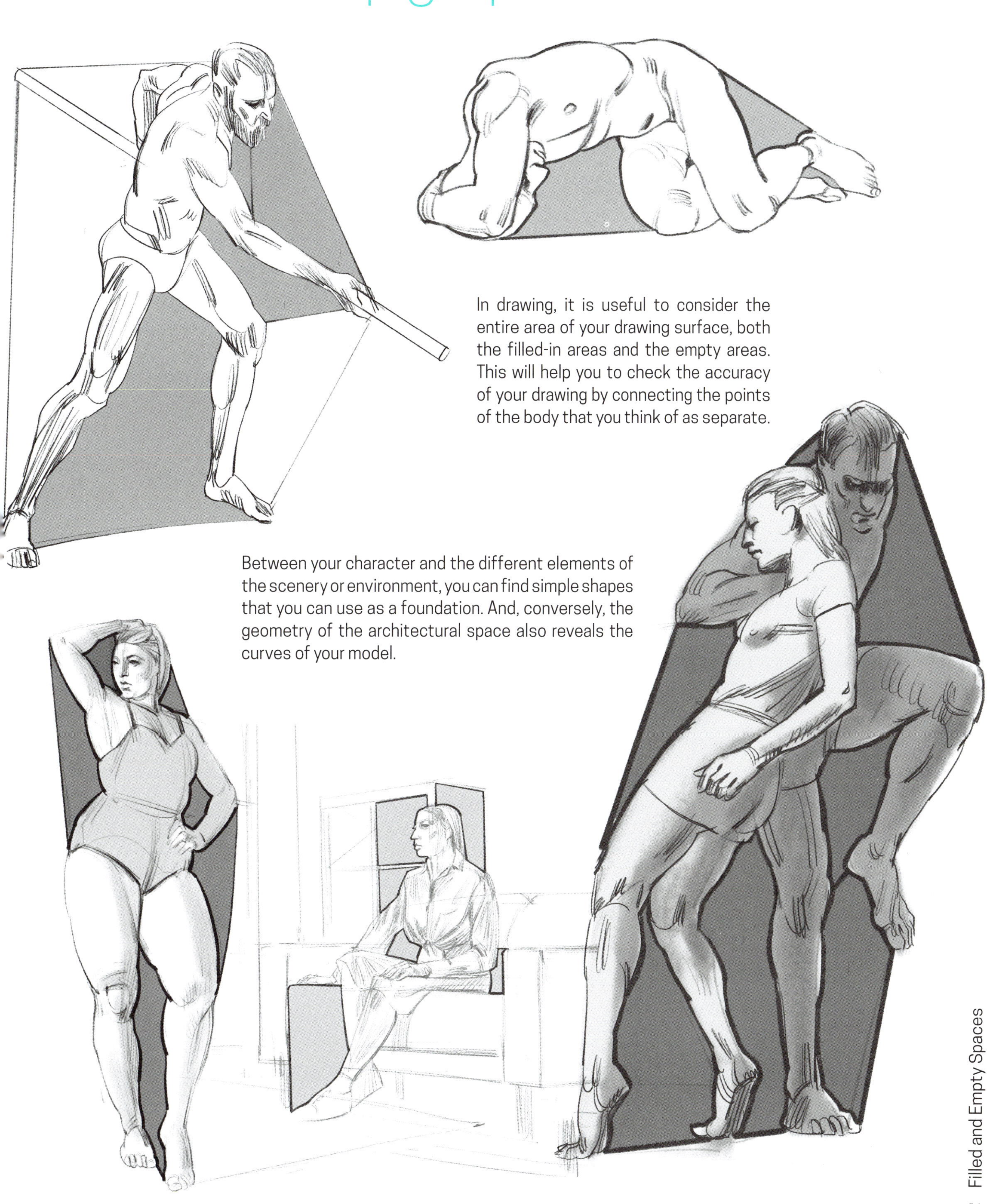

In drawing, it is useful to consider the entire area of your drawing surface, both the filled-in areas and the empty areas. This will help you to check the accuracy of your drawing by connecting the points of the body that you think of as separate.

Between your character and the different elements of the scenery or environment, you can find simple shapes that you can use as a foundation. And, conversely, the geometry of the architectural space also reveals the curves of your model.

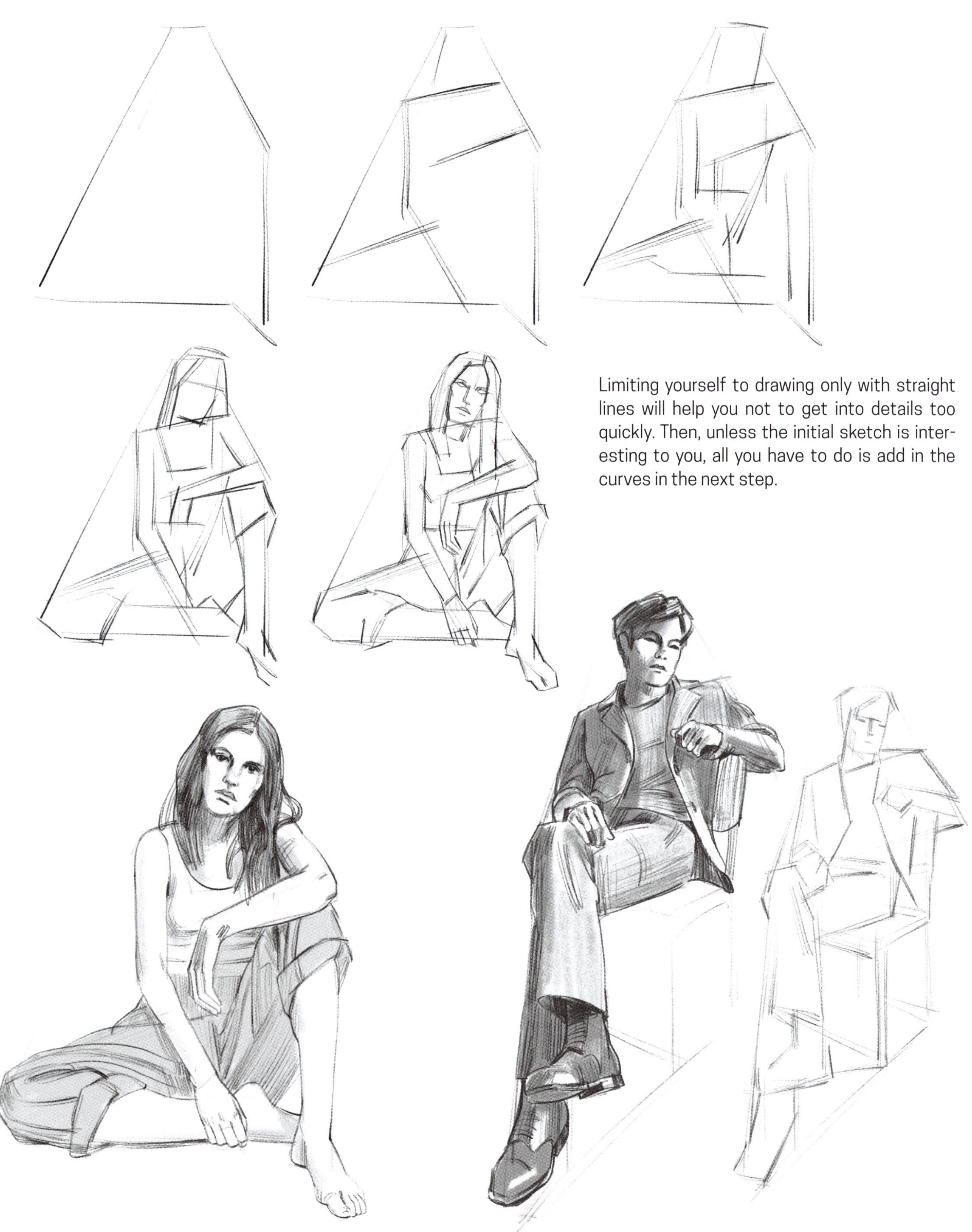

Limiting yourself to drawing only with straight lines will help you not to get into details too quickly. Then, unless the initial sketch is interesting to you, all you have to do is add in the curves in the next step.

Alignments

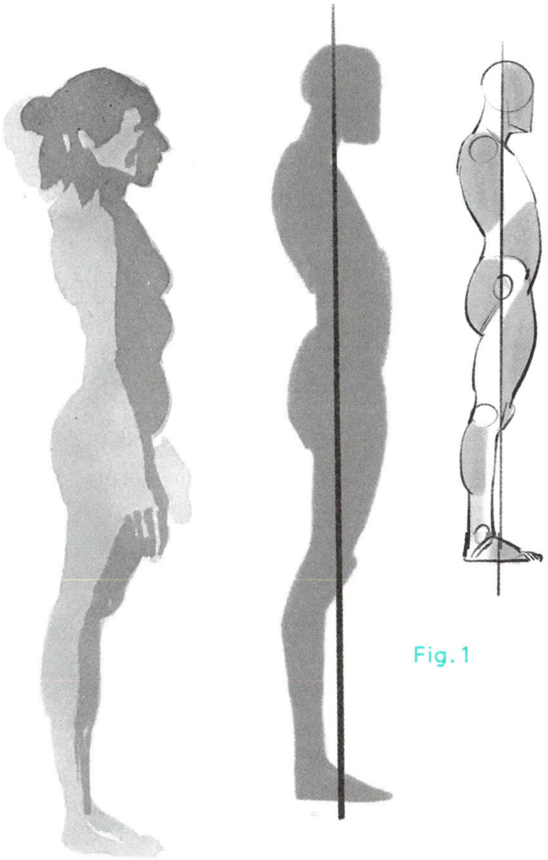

Fig. 1 To account for the balance and weight of a body, imagine its segments as being alternately distributed first on one side and then the other of a vertical line (see also the vertical line on p. 12).

A weight being carried at the end of the arm or on the back will force a change in the posture and vertical alignments.

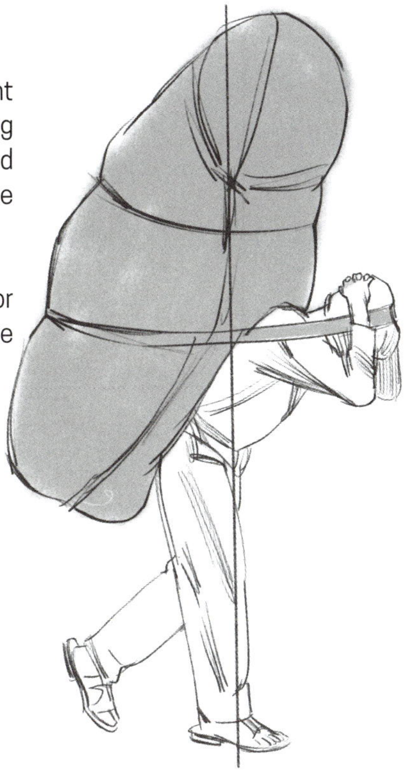

Fig. 3 Drawing following Paul Richer (see the resources on p. 32).

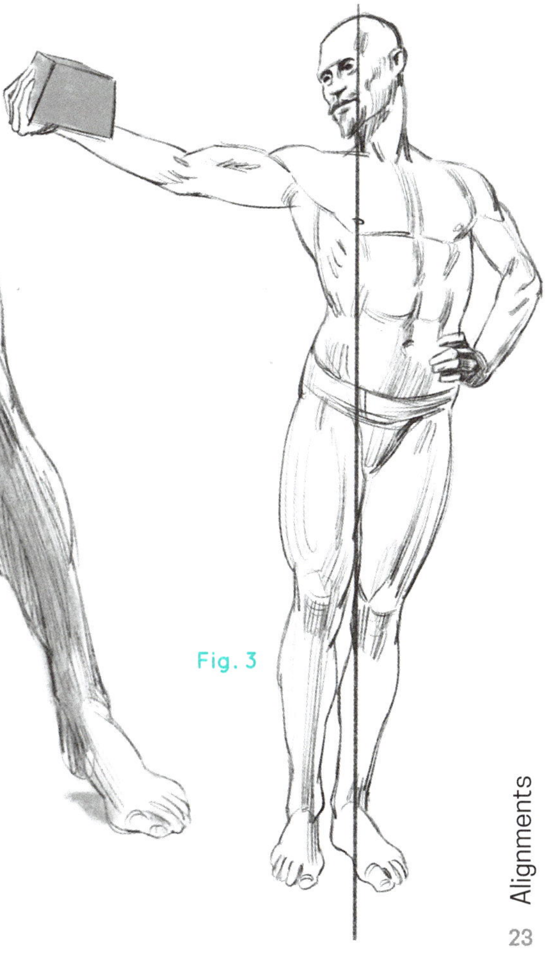

Fig. 2 In a posture with one hip out, the weight of the body is placed on the supporting leg (drawing following Michelangelo).

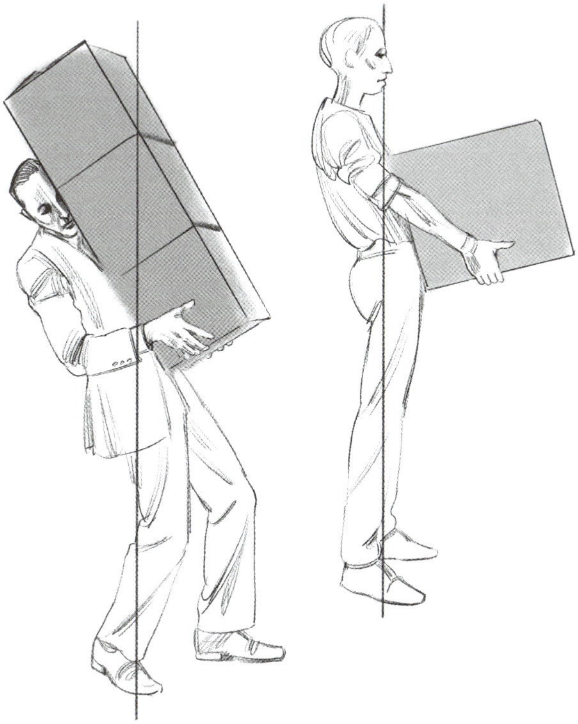

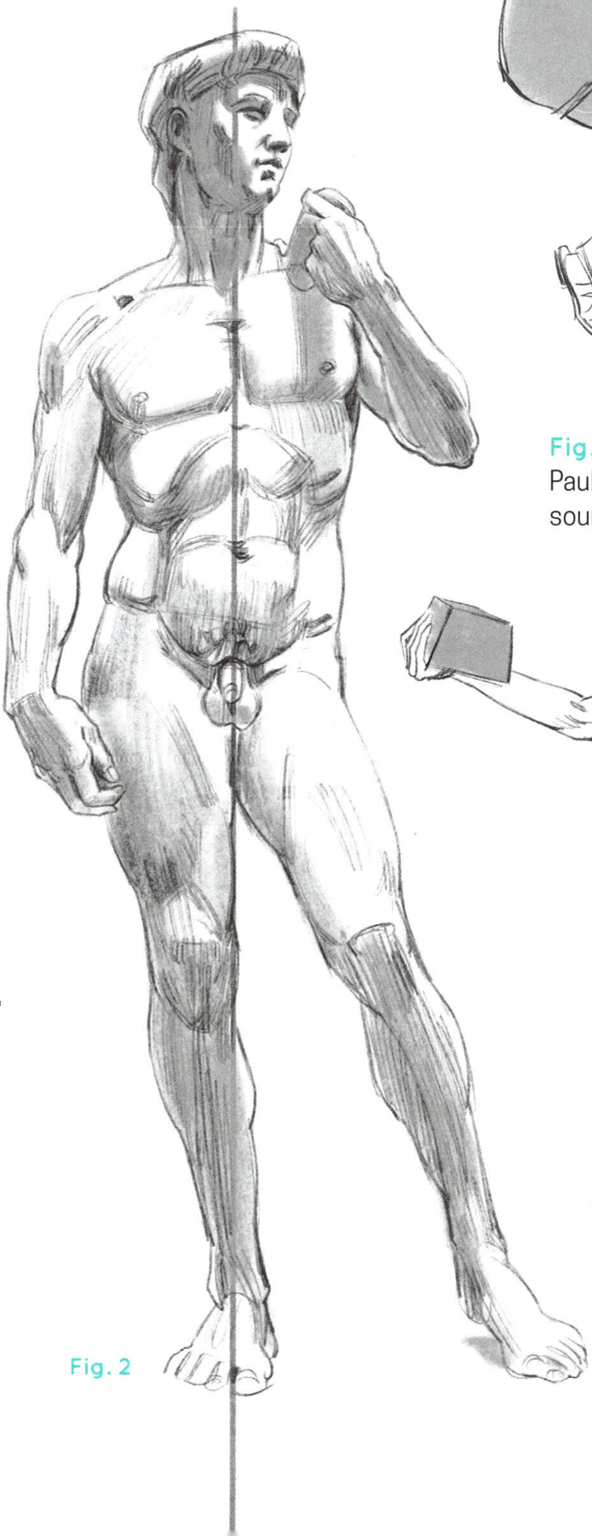

Outlines and Continuous Lines

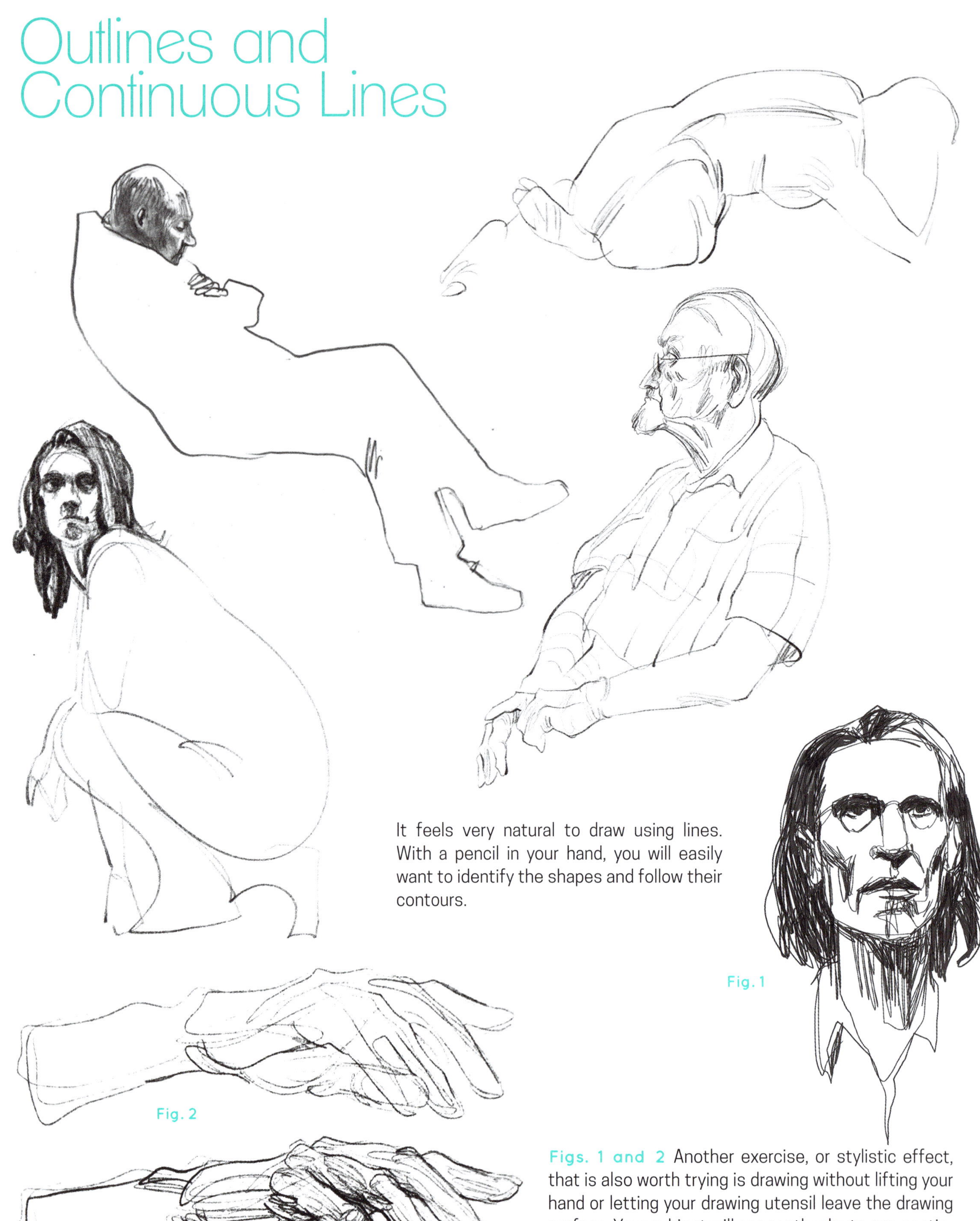

It feels very natural to draw using lines. With a pencil in your hand, you will easily want to identify the shapes and follow their contours.

Figs. 1 and 2 Another exercise, or stylistic effect, that is also worth trying is drawing without lifting your hand or letting your drawing utensil leave the drawing surface. Your subject will appear thanks to one continuous line; don't be afraid of scribbling or having your lines overlap.

Key Lines

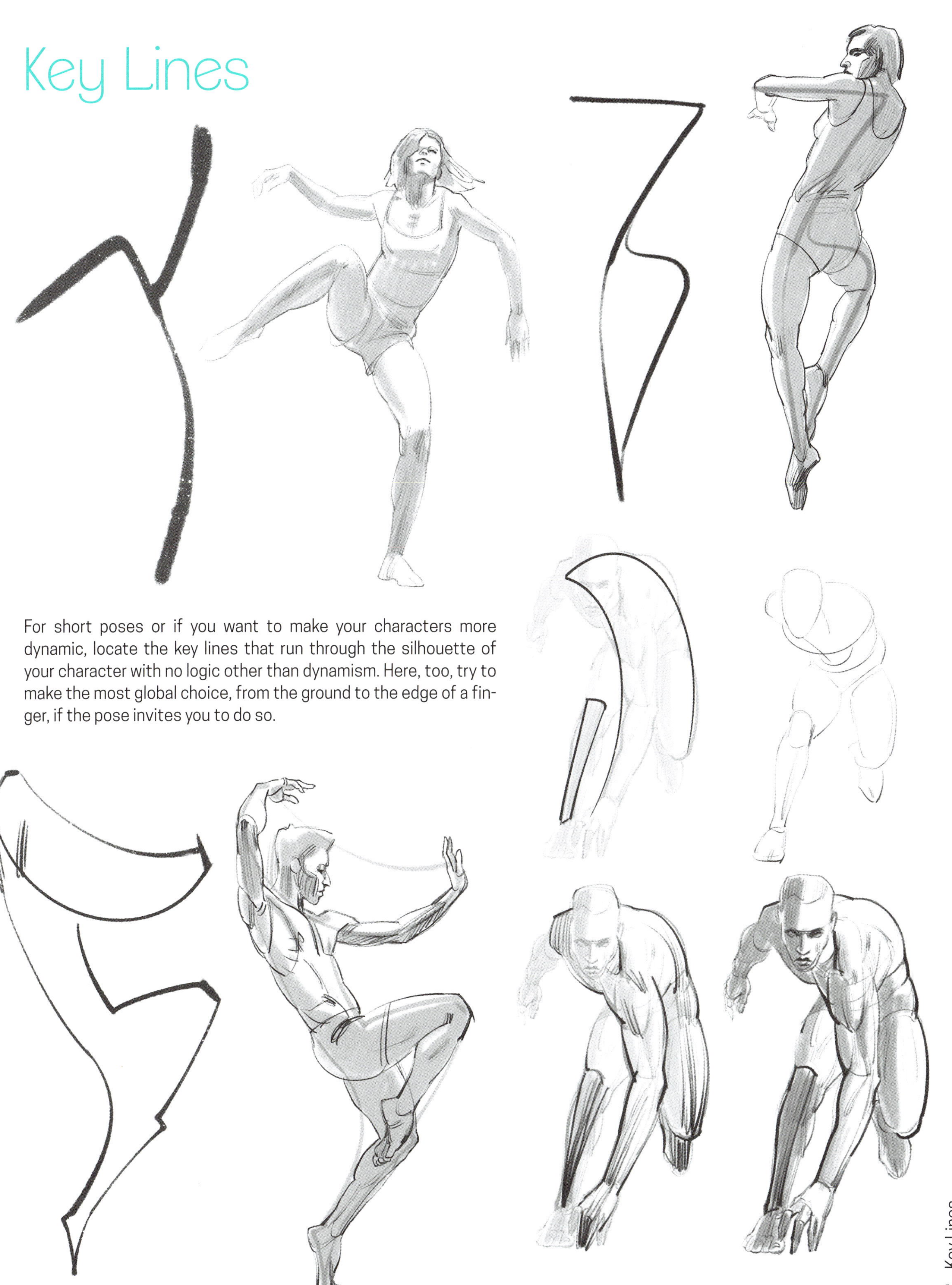

For short poses or if you want to make your characters more dynamic, locate the key lines that run through the silhouette of your character with no logic other than dynamism. Here, too, try to make the most global choice, from the ground to the edge of a finger, if the pose invites you to do so.

Perspective

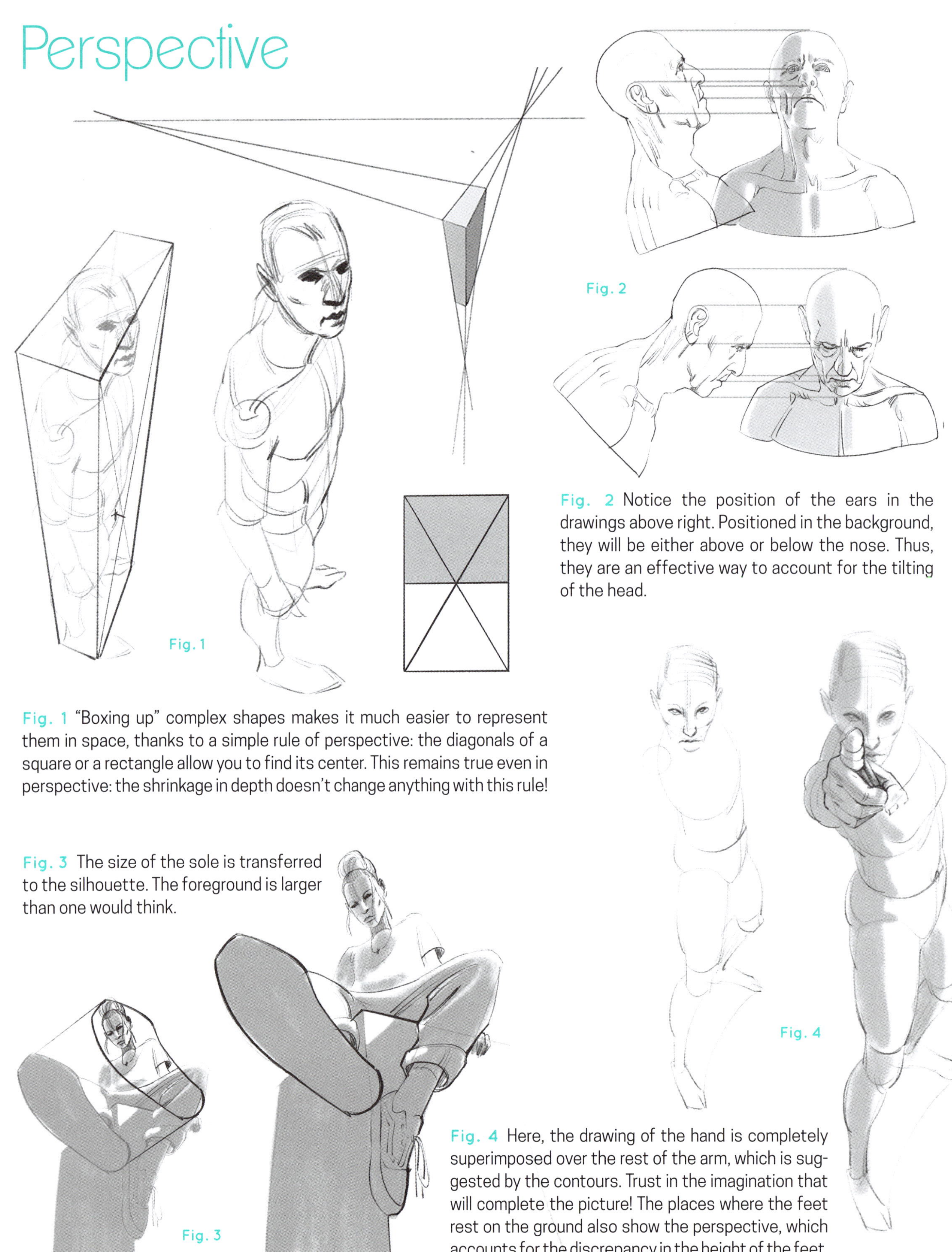

Fig. 1 "Boxing up" complex shapes makes it much easier to represent them in space, thanks to a simple rule of perspective: the diagonals of a square or a rectangle allow you to find its center. This remains true even in perspective: the shrinkage in depth doesn't change anything with this rule!

Fig. 2 Notice the position of the ears in the drawings above right. Positioned in the background, they will be either above or below the nose. Thus, they are an effective way to account for the tilting of the head.

Fig. 3 The size of the sole is transferred to the silhouette. The foreground is larger than one would think.

Fig. 4 Here, the drawing of the hand is completely superimposed over the rest of the arm, which is suggested by the contours. Trust in the imagination that will complete the picture! The places where the feet rest on the ground also show the perspective, which accounts for the discrepancy in the height of the feet.

Foreshortening

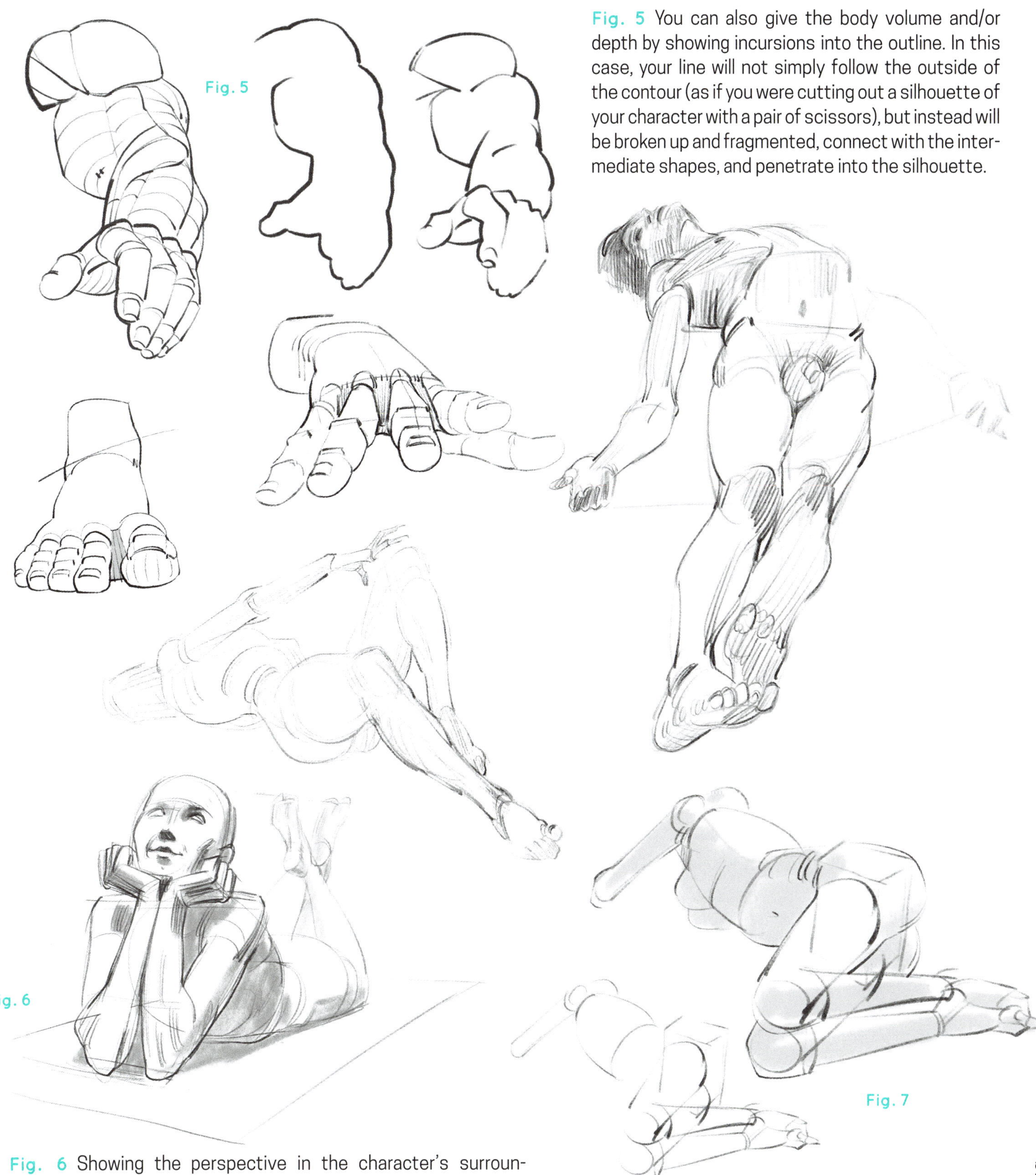

Fig. 5 You can also give the body volume and/or depth by showing incursions into the outline. In this case, your line will not simply follow the outside of the contour (as if you were cutting out a silhouette of your character with a pair of scissors), but instead will be broken up and fragmented, connect with the intermediate shapes, and penetrate into the silhouette.

Fig. 6 Showing the perspective in the character's surroundings—a rug, the lines of a parquet floor, the general volume of a room, etc.—reinforces our perception of depth. This is also the case when we emphasize the foreground—for instance, by pressing harder on the pencil.

Fig. 7 Stacking and superimposing simple volumes on top of each other can facilitate the demonstration of foreshortening (see also pp. 18 and 19).

Light Values

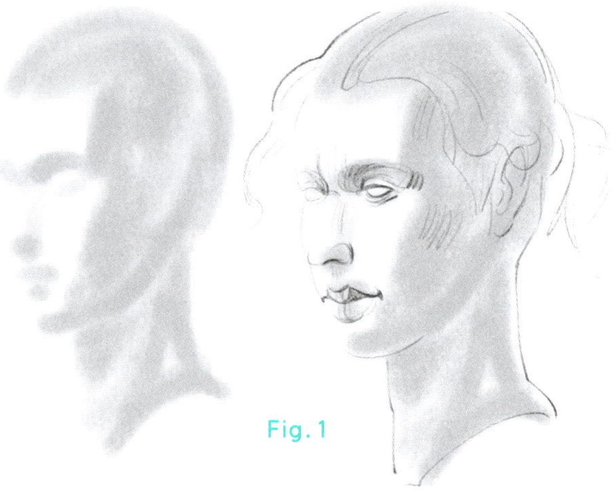

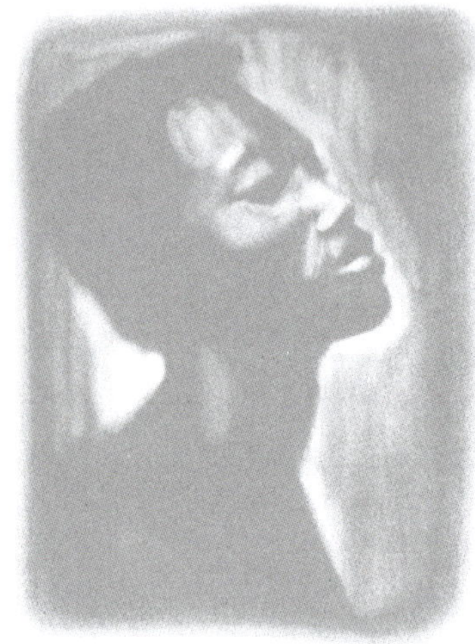

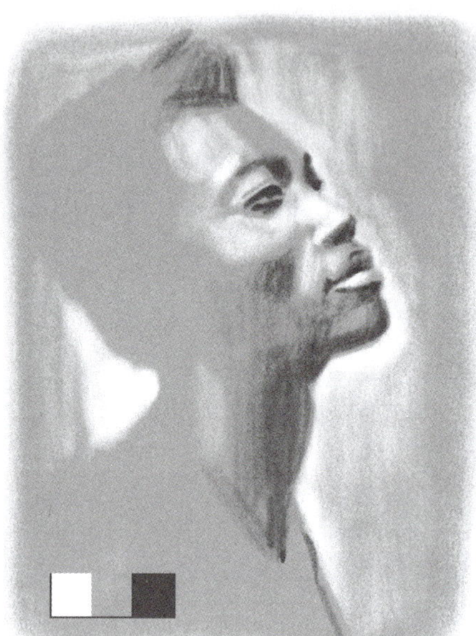

Fig. 1

Fig. 2

Fig. 1 You can work with light values—with the interplay of shadows and light—from the very beginning by placing the shadows first (or the highlights, if you are using dark paper).

Fig. 2 If you intend to work with light values in more depth, I recommend that you decide on a shading chart in advance, by drawing a small checkerboard in the margin of your drawing, running from white to black (or dark gray, if you choose), and that you then stick to this range of shades for the duration of this exercise. In other words, decide in advance in which of the squares of the checkerboard (i.e., using which shade) you will position each of the different tones and infinite variations of gray that your eye will perceive on the skin and/or the clothing of your model.

I suggest that you start by applying the medium gray. Because white will be the color of your foundation (assuming that your paper is white), you should not even touch the areas of light—this is called "reserve white." If your foundation is gray, as in the case shown here, then you will have to erase the white areas. Then, finally, end with the darkest tone.

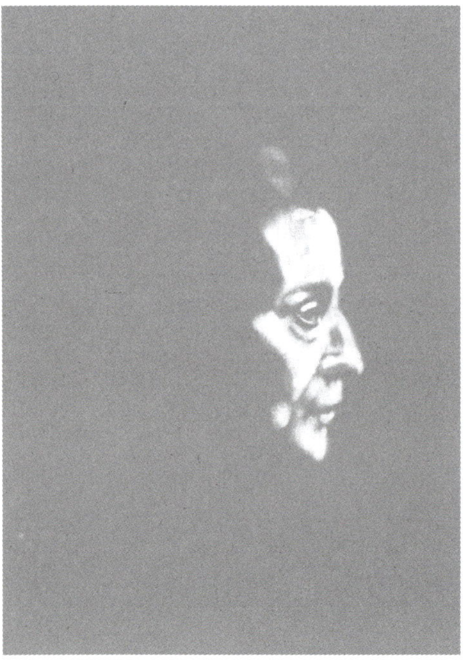

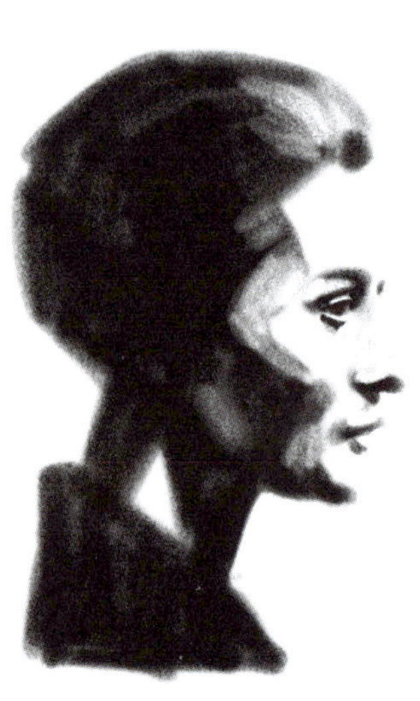

Fig. 3

Fig. 3 Superimposing two layers on a graphics tablet. The lights are drawn with an eraser on a gray background, which corresponds to the medium gray of the shading chart.

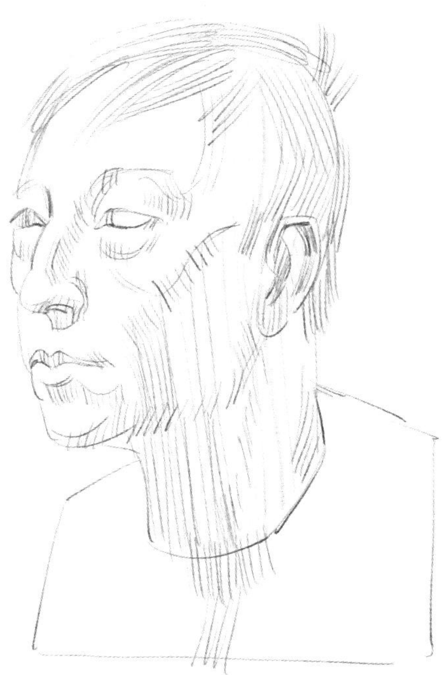 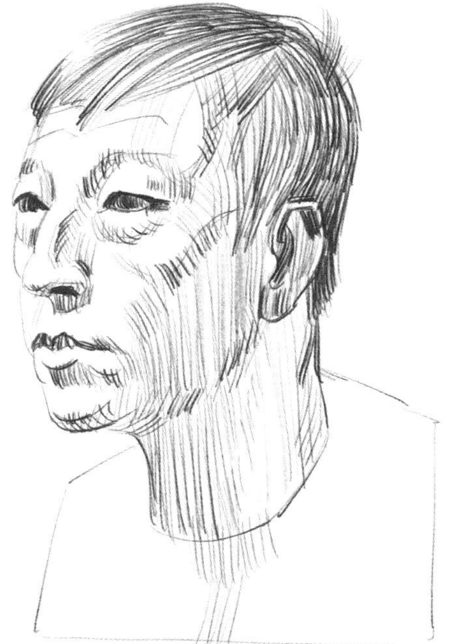 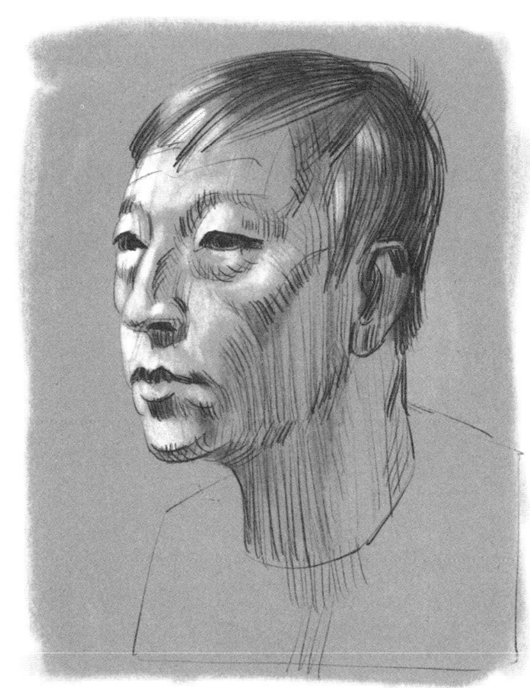

Drawing with lines matches up very nicely with indications of light values. You can choose to express the volume in the way that engravers do, solely by using tighter or looser networks of intersecting lines.

You can also choose between strong contrasts or staying within the shades of gray.

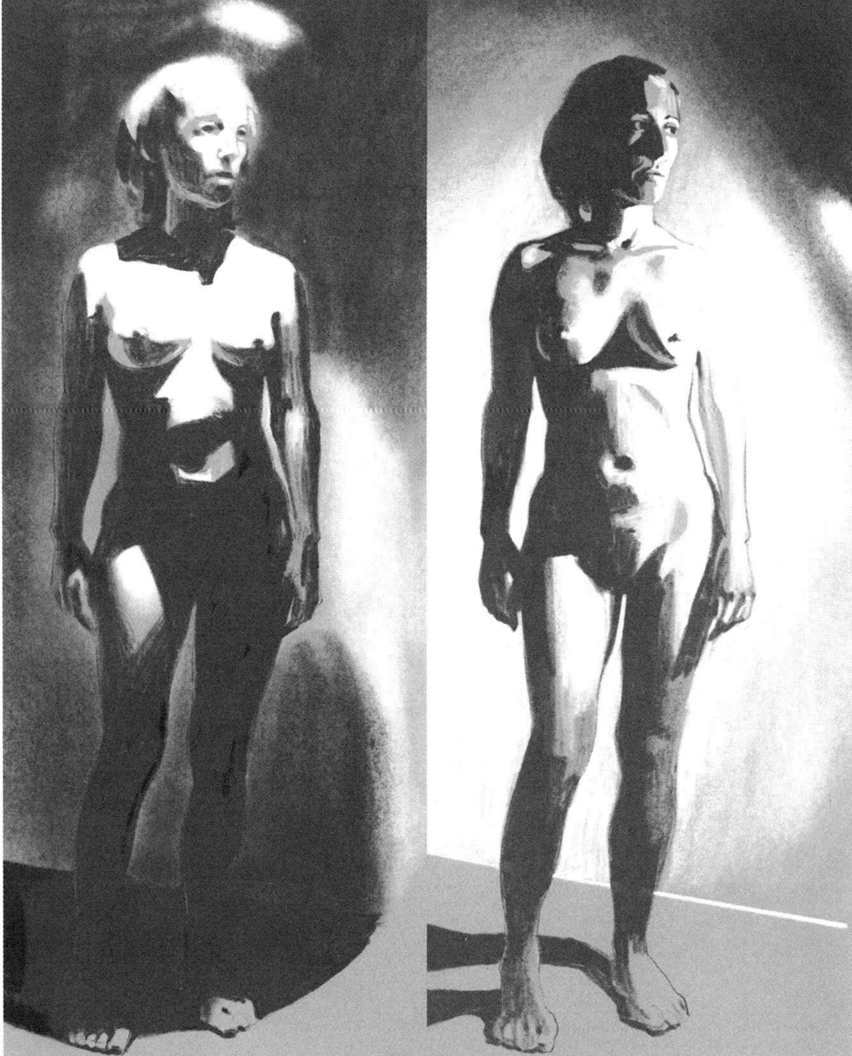

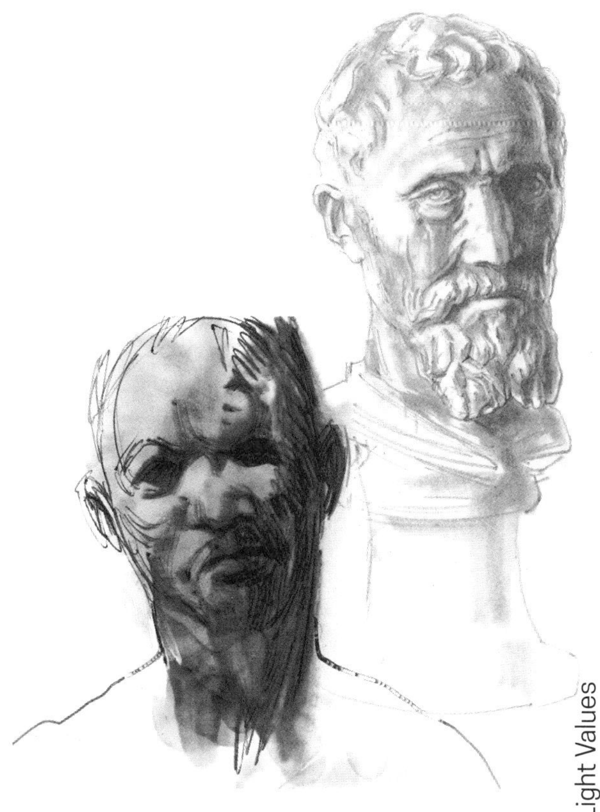

Garment Folds

We can distinguish among three different cases here: the fabric can either hang (Fig. 1), be stretched taut (Figs. 2, 3, and 4), or fall (Fig. 5).

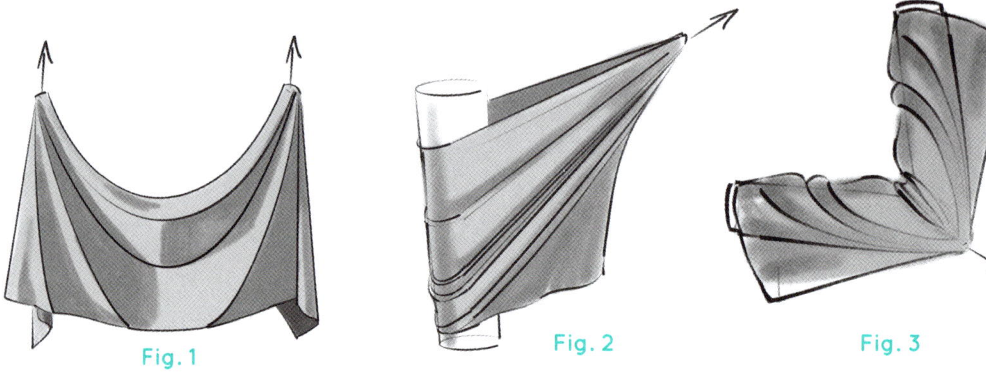

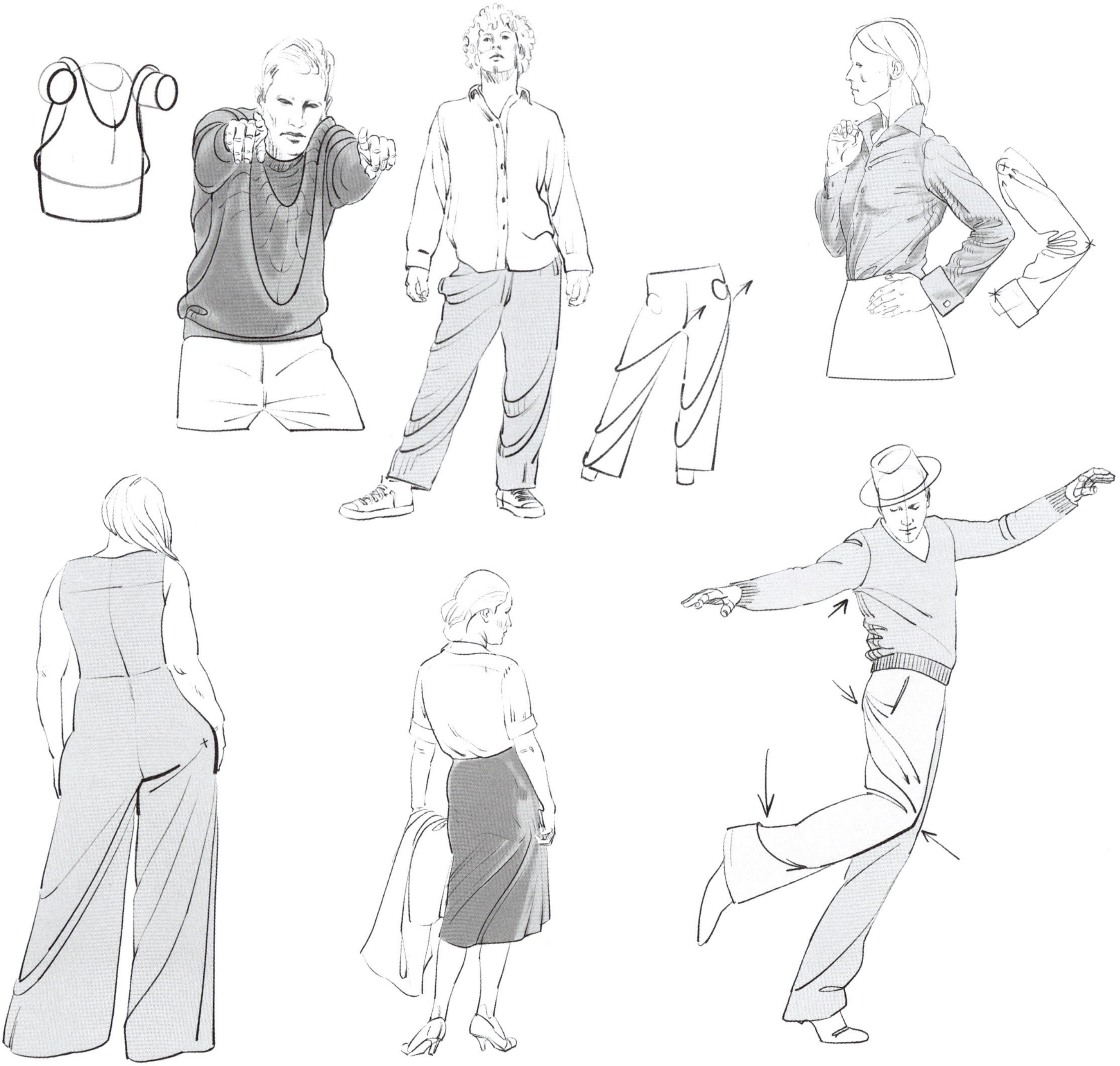

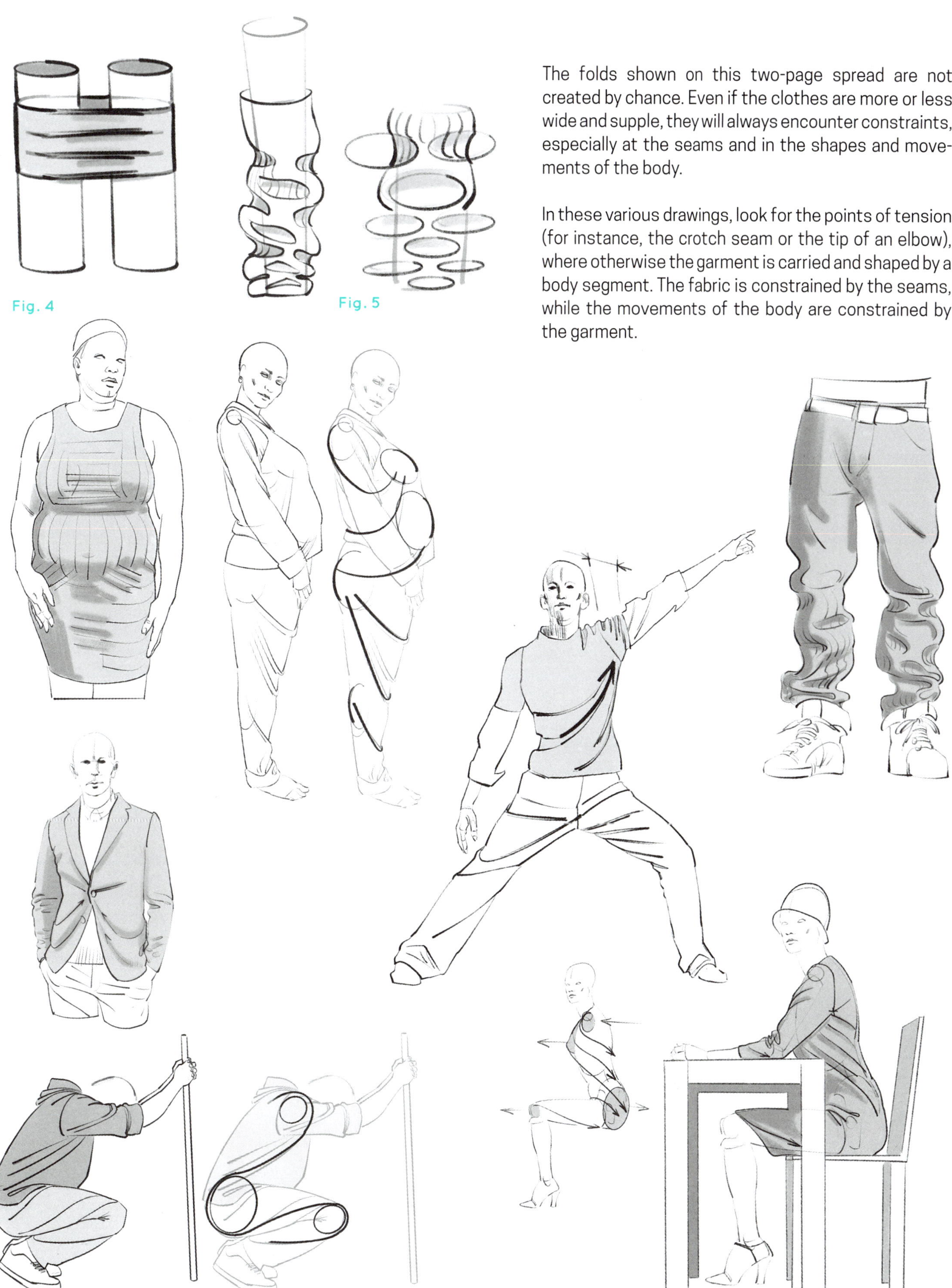

Fig. 4

Fig. 5

The folds shown on this two-page spread are not created by chance. Even if the clothes are more or less wide and supple, they will always encounter constraints, especially at the seams and in the shapes and movements of the body.

In these various drawings, look for the points of tension (for instance, the crotch seam or the tip of an elbow), where otherwise the garment is carried and shaped by a body segment. The fabric is constrained by the seams, while the movements of the body are constrained by the garment.

Resources

By the same author:

The *Morpho* drawing series

Robert Barrett, *Life Drawing: How To Portray the Figure with Accuracy and Expression*, North Light Books

Jake Spicer, *Figure Drawing: A Complete Guide to Drawing the Human Body*, Ilex Press

For French speakers (from the original French edition):

Gottfried Bammes, *Der nackte Mensch. Hand- und Lehrbuch der Anatomie für Künstler*, Verlag der Kunst Dresden

Thomas Wienc, *Dessiner d'après modèle vivant*, Éditions Dessain et Tolra

The works of Paul Richer are available at Gallica.bnf.fr

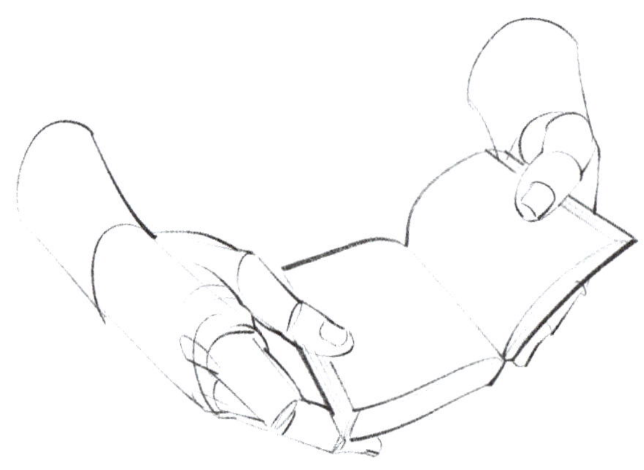